Menageries of Melanin

A selection of essays and quotes of S. Quanaah

~Quanaah Publishing~

Quanaah Publishing

www.quanaah-publishing.com

Menageries of Melanin
©Copyright 2017
Quanaah Publishing

Written/Edited by S. Quanaah
Cover Design by S. Quanaah

-FOR TRAINING AND PUBLIC SPEAKING INFO-

S. Quanaah
EMAIL: atlantisbuild@gmail.com

www.atlantisschool.blogspot.com
www.youtube.com/quanaah
www.soundcloud.com/atlantisbuild

Printed in
The United States of America

Menageries of Melanin

Dedicated to my Father Philip B. Frank, the man
who started me on my journey of self knowledge

Introduction

A menagerie is a collection of wild animals kept in captivity for exhibition; a strange or diverse collection of people or things. This book is a series of essays and quotes pertaining to the black experience. To some, this experience is nothing more than a menagerie of melanin. To others, we are a small percentage of solutionaries forging our world of cultural freedom.

-S. Quanaah

College Access
Setting The Course

On Saturday August 13th, 2016 I had the pleasure of attending a College Simulation Experience to speak on a panel for high school youth about the importance of Self Advocacy and role of Social Justice. The College Simulation Experience is an initiative dedicated to improving college retention rates for students from disadvantaged backgrounds. This stylized enactment of college life used dramatic role playing to help pre-college students develop time management and financial management skills, as well as better understand the responsibilities associated with collegiate success. For the last two decades I've worked with youth, from preschoolers to college age students. Of my many experiences one of the most alarming has been the lack of career preparedness on the part of our young boys of color. It's been quite common for me to talk to a young man who is finishing his junior year or in the middle of his senior year of high school with a desire to go to college with no knowledge of the SAT; an entrance exam created by the College Board that's used by most colleges and universities to make admissions decisions. When I say no knowledge I'm talking about they never even heard of it before. On a couple of occasions, I've had this conversation with young men with their parents and the parents didn't know what the SAT was either. My response? I began to educate them, and youth as early as elementary school, about college access and provide them with the resources so they're successful in their undertakings. One project I did was the A.S.I.A. College Tour Project which enabled me to sponsor two high school students on a black college tour. In recent years I learned about another subject we need to be educated about in regards to college access and that is the trending concept of *Previewing* and *Forward Credit* summer school classes.

Previewing and Forward Credit Summer Classes are classes offered by high schools for students who are striving to get a head start on a class they'll be taking next year or to earn credit for a class they won't need to take next year. One of the sixth graders in my STYA Program actually earned Forward Credit this year taking a math and science class this summer before he starts middle school in the autumn. Students also take summer classes to accumulate AP [Advanced Placement] class credit because College Admission Boards look at AP exams. In many cities college access has become so competitive that high schools often hold summer school lotteries for students to be admitted to their programs. Many of these programs such as Northfield Mount Hermon in Massachusetts have tuition costs of $2,900 per day and $3,700 when English is a second language. Horace Mann School in Pelon [Bronx] offered a summer physics class to students for $4,175 and the Hun School of Princeton in New Jerusalem [New Jersey] offered boarding tuition for $5,675 this year. Therein lies a problem that widens a disparity that already exists between students who can afford this and low income students; low income students simply don't have access to these summer school programs and an opportunity to preview or earn forward credit for classes next year. low income students already find it difficult to compete and this puts them even further behind unless we can help supplement their access to creative ways. This is also important in terms of encouraging our youth to explore the trades and entrepreneurship as viable alternatives. Not because they can't compete but because data supports the fact that many of these students competing for college access usually don't settle into a career path that's in alignment with the degree and debt they spent their life paying for.

My young Queens don't come from a place of financial access where their mother and I had/have the kind of disposable income to pay for the college access other parents could. We've had to canvass the landscape to find any and every program available to give them an advantage to academically compete with those parents who could send two to three of their children to a Hun School of Princeton for summer without robbing Peter to pay Paul. This has also been challenging because we co-parent our Queens and reside in different states. Canvassing that landscape resulted in finding free SAT classes being offered on Saturdays, taking them on college tours, doing community service, networking to gain access to resources and enrolling them in programs such as project Forward Leap. We also encouraged them to explore high school sports or extracurricular activities they'd like which would could result in a partial or full scholarship to college. My eldest Queen Asiyah played lacrosse in high school and successfully earned an athletic scholarship to Howard University to play lacrosse; ranked #2 among all Black College and Universities by U.S. News and World Report. She's a senior this year and has been awarded Defense of Player of the Year twice. My youngest Queen Aziza also attends Howard and is in her sophomore year. She's 19 now and I have a picture of her wearing a Howard U shirt when she was 8 years old; which says a lot about her vision and ability to execute her plan to reach her goal. Although we as parents helped provide them with resources, encouragement and access to experiences to expand their mind and its possibilities, it was/is ultimately up to them to be self-determined and discipline enough to set forth a plan to reach their goals. It's their life, not ours and we're proud to see them evolve into young women.

As parents, we are like many parents who simply didn't or don't have the money to do certain things for our children that others could. What we didn't or don't have financially we learned to find or create. For example, every year since our Queens have been in college they've attended summer school to earn Forward Credit for college. They didn't have to pay for these classes because their ole Earth works Administration at a college where they could take these classes tuition free. We learned creative ways to help our children gain access to those resources and I've likewise shared these creative ways with parents and youth I've worked with over the years. While this is a start this definitely isn't enough and cannot replace actual credit hours many privileged students are literally buying during the summer to bolster their high school transcripts and earn free transportation to college. Even though The No Child Left Behind Act signed into law by George W. Bush over a decade ago [2002] under its Title One was established to distribute funding to schools and school districts with a high percentage of students from low-income families, funding needs to be directed to assist these students seeking to Preview and earn Forward Credit during School Classes. This funding is initially distributed to state educational agencies who then allocate those funds to local education agencies that invest those funds to public schools in need. This means that it will require active Parent/Teacher Associations and other Lobby Groups to work with local city and county elected officials who can leverage state officials to address this disparity. If you're already living in a school district where schools are already in need there is already funding being directed to those schools under the guise of No Child Left Behind. Therefore, the goal is simply a redirection of funding already there to help improve college access and retention rates for disadvantaged students by offering SAT/ACT classes and practice exams, scholarships for students seeking Forward Credit in Summer Classes and even transportation to other schools in the district that programs that will help close the college access gap.

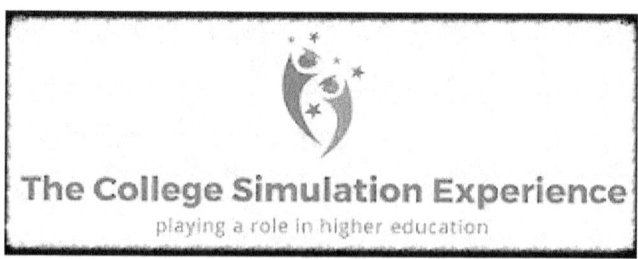

The College Simulation Experience
playing a role in higher education

In closing, whether you have children or not, you may have nieces, nephews, cousins or friends with children who need to understand this changing academic landscape in America where youth are no longer being sentenced to summer school for failing but choosing to go, and paying money, just to get ahead. This is setting the tone for the level of competitiveness within our future global market and the power dynamics between the Haves and Havenots. If we're not in a financial position for our children to formally Preview a class next year then we need to find out what they will be learning and have them enrolled in some program, find a tutor, tutor them ourselves or explore other creative ways to keep them academically competitive so they don't fall behind their peers. If we don't personally have the financial ability to help them enroll in summer classes to earn Forward Credit then we must consider creative ways to finance it such as crowdfunding, gofundme and etc. There are also organizations and agencies that provide scholarships to support youth like this. We gotta canvass the landscape! Many of our children aren't college bound and they also need to know that it's O.K., everybody isn't. However, they also must understand that they must have a career alternative such as learning a trades and being an entrepreneur. If they're not striving to legitimately eat to bring something to the table or build their own table they will be on someone's menu.

Understanding

Understanding is seeing people, places and things for what they are, NOT what "they appear" to be. For example, you appear to be an individual yet you're really a composite of all of your ancestors who came before you. You are the sum total of what was and what you choose to be. This is the reason the babies or understanding is the best part. They are born as the composite of what was and the infinite potential to produce the best that we are yet to see!

Social Networthing

The purpose of social networking should be to increase and share our social capital.

P.E.A.C.E.

P- Possibilities
E- Enhance
A- A
C- Child's
E- Evolution

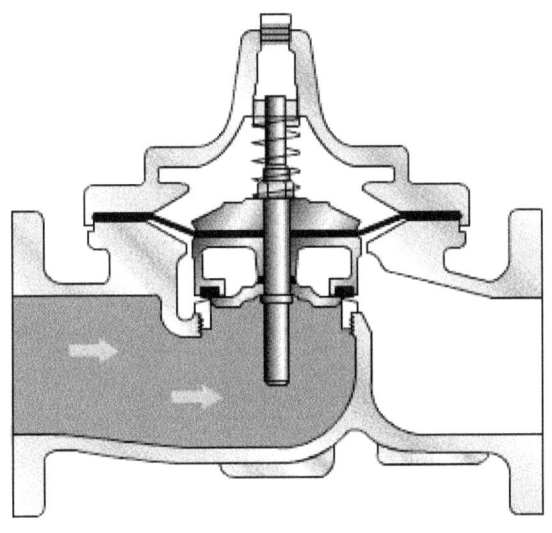

Relief Valveology (RV)

I recently had a dream about how systems work, or don't work, based upon a role of a relief valve. Over the years I've watched the ebb and flow of important issues within the mainstream media and various talking heads weigh in on everything from #BlackLivesMatter, police brutality, foreign policy, the 2016 Election and Monsanto to the show Empire, Caitlyn Jenner, LHHATL, Raven Symone and McDonalds offering breakfast All Day. While some of these critical perspectives and the dissatisfaction is genuine, I think many of them serve as valves to simply release pressure on "the system", not to fundamentally change anything.

So what is a relief valve (RV)? A relief valve (RV) is a gate-like device used to control or limit the pressure on a system or vessel that can cause that system's equipment to fail and become damaged. The valve is designed to safeguard a system by limiting the maximum amount of pressure on that system. To relieve that pressure the valve opens. When pressure conditions return to normal, the valve close. Without a relief valve pressure will continue to grow until other components in the system fail, thus ultimately relieving that pressure.

Sound familiar? Have you ever listened to the perspectives of some people and see that their underlying intent is safeguarding the system/status quo? What about those who function like a valve; they open [their mouth] to speak out on issues the people are dissatisfied about, yet close [their mouth] when the pressure to change those conditions returns back to normal? In Freemasonry this is the same role and responsibility of the Tiler/Tyler; a gate-keeper and symbolic valve used to [safe]guard the outer door to the lodge from potentially malicious, unqualified and nosey people. Tiler comes from the Latin word "*tegere*" which means 'to cover' or roof. In other words, this is a person who got the system covered... Although some of these people you see organizing rallies in cities, doing lectures, sharing videos and etc. may not be due paying members of a masonic lodge, they act as Tilers none the less. I elaborate on Tilers and other things in my latest book Eyes Wide Shut: The Science of Secret Societies. While some may even be on the government's payroll to quell the emotions of the public who are putting pressure on changing public policy, some are not but they both serve the purpose of maintaining the status quo. Keep in mind that I am not talking about Don Lemon or those who come from the David Clarke tribe. We know their posture and it's not to release the pressure building up within black/brown communities. It's obvious that they, and others, are here to safeguard the system that's already failing in many areas. I'm referring to those some of us assume are for a new system of things. I'm talking about some of these black militant, black conscious, nationalistic, religious, Pan-African, metaphysician, sovereign folks who appear to be banging on the system. I'm also talking about some of these white liberal, free-range, off the grid, anarchist, racism conference attending, political candidate Eminemians who appear to be banging on the system too. Some of them, are only here, to provide vent forums. And once you've gotten your concerns off of your chest while they nod their heads and articulate they understand, things remain the same. And if you ask too many questions, get deemed unqualified or accused of entertaining malicious intents against them or their leaders, you'll see the Tiler come out.

At the end of the day we must be mindful that some people are simply not invested in being change agents to help transform the conditions of this world. They're nothing more than relief valves that helps release the pressure being put on this system. It doesn't matter what gender, ethnicity, religion, sexual orientation they are; they're all gate keepers. Age also doesn't matter because the older ones strive to socialize and incentivize the younger generation to do the same thing. There are some things right about what goes on here in America in comparison to other places in the world. There are also things that aren't right that needed to be changed yesterday, perhaps many years ago. In order to do this, knowledge must be our foundation, not sentimentality, being in our feelings or getting riled up to rally around talking heads who aren't invested in change. The more we know, the more we can personally and collectively do n order to see the changes in our families, communities and society as a whole.

It's not about valve-like position aspirations or being proud that we're the only person of color on our job. The only pride in being a gate-keeper is safeguarding the lives of the most vulnerable members of our society; our youth, elders, women, disabled, disenfranchised and poor. And it shouldn't take pressure from these segments of our population to make changes in the way this system operates. When we don't, that pressure will continue to grow until other components in the system, including the system itself, will fail. It's not rocket science, I'm simply talking about relief valves.

TIME

Time is the great tester and offers the best testimonial of our techniques.

Knowledge Of Self

Knowledge Of Self [KOS] is more than just personal growth and development, it's the positive relationships we forge through interpersonal growth and development!

America, The Beautiful?

It's been 10 days since the police murders of Alton Sterling, Philando Castile, the hanging of Michael George Smith Jr. and the deaths of 5 Dallas police officers. I wanted to take some time to work through my emotions and gather my thoughts before I shared them with all of you here. Let me start by saying that in times like this especially, our greatest resource and sense of clarity is in our youth. As Five Percenters we view them as the understanding and symbolic to a star: dispelling the darkness with the light of truth that's often light years from where many of us presently stand. I'm currently facilitating my STYA Summer Enrichment Program for 5 weeks and even though we've discussed these incidents they've helped me work through my emotions and make sense out of what I've been seeing. If you find yourself in a similar place I would encourage you to invest some quality time with our youth as well. Black people make up about 12% of the U.S. population while White People make up 63% of the U.S. population. With that mind, here are some statistics I want to bring to your attention:

- Black people make up about 60% of the prison population.
- 1 out of 3 black men will go to jail in their lifetime.
- 70% of school related arrests or referrals to law enforcement are people of color.
- From 1980-2007, 1 out of 3 25 million adults arrested for drugs were black.
- Based upon population, of the 752 police deaths in 2015 blacks are 2 1/2 times more likely to be shot by police.

Statistically there are many other racial disparities in regards to income, education, health, legislation and etc. These and other inequalities highlight the unstable quicksand like socioeconomic landscape that not just black people but all people in this country live upon. It's important to articulate that because some people are under the impression that whatever happens to 12% of the U.S. population has nothing to do with them, as if these lives don't matter. As I always say to people who brush things off that are happening on the other side of the world, the other side of their country, the other side of their state/province and the other side of town: be mindful because that can eventually be in your backyard.

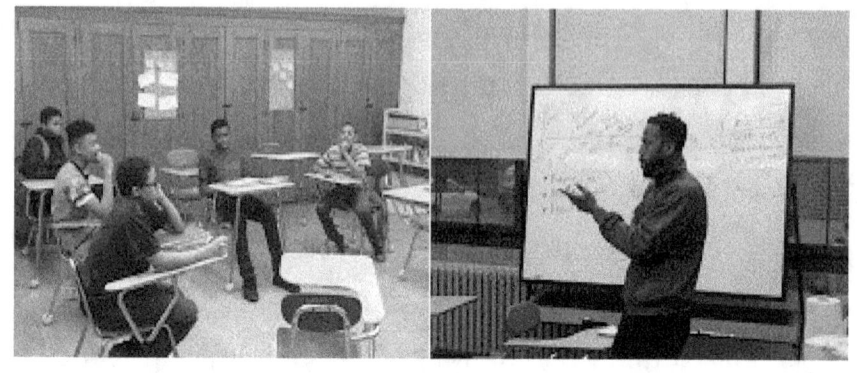

Of those disparities, one of the greatest concerns black people have historically had within America is with its law enforcement. Several months ago on December 18th and 21st of 2015 I had an opportunity to do a workshop with young men at Gaskill Middle School about the history of law enforcement in this country. The first and most important thing to understand about law enforcement is that it was never created to protect and serve black people or any people of color. In fact, law enforcement was created to maintain order, enforce law and protect the property of those who established it. Back in 1555 when millions of black people were brought to America via the Trans-Atlantic Slave Trade, white slave masters organized the first Slave Patrols to maintain order, enforce law and protect their plantations. These Slave Patrols in the South and Night Watchmen in the North evolved into police forces by the 1800s. The city of Boston is credited with organizing the first formal police force in 1830; a generation before slavery legally ended and slavery by another name began as a prison industrial complex via a ratified 13th Amendment. Again, these slave patrols, night watchmen and police forces were created to maintain the social order, enforce the laws and protect the property of the ruling class, which were not black and other people of color. The only difference in this power dynamic today is the militarization of these police forces across America. If there is any truth to the law enforcement adage "Protect & Serve", it clearly has not historically applied to black people. This is the reason many people have and are advocating fundamental reforms in law enforcement and the criminal justice system; it was never created by or for the benefit of black people or any people of color in the first place. Since America's 1776 inception, its Founding Fathers formed a republic governed with politicians who forged policies that were protected by slave patrols and eventually the police. This begs the question that many of us continue to ask: How can we expect to get justice from an unjust system?

Systemically, some things have not and will not change. Other things can be changed. Sometimes the system itself needs to be revamped. Depending upon the demographics and socioeconomic landscape of one's region and local city, systemic changes and the degree of resistance will vary. Some people may not consider that. In my city our local police force were one of the first in the country to invest in body cameras, without a bunch of prompting or protesting from the community. While there are many national similarities across the board in regards to racial disparities, police violence and inequalities, we must also take into account the regional and local similarities and differences. There is no silver bullet or one size fits all approach to address these issues and the sooner we understand that the better equipped we are to help resolve these issues. I recently saw a BLM Chapter in Minnesota calling for the disbandment of their local police force. That may be an effective approach where they live, not where you live.

In closing a want to offer seven points to consider wherever we may be in the U.S. or in other countries experiencing some of the same racial disparities, police violence and inequalities.

1. Environmentally there are no boundaries for consciousness; this is why so much is invested in media that socially engineers narratives that distracts, deceives, confuses and emotionally destabilizes the people. The largest investment in any country is not its military it's their media. The media is the conduit of its cultural ideas and icons; their greatest export that their military ultimately protects. I've said this numerous times and I will continue to say it: we must use our platform to CONSISTENTLY control the narrative and amplify our voice. Facebook Live and Periscope have been a great resource people are now using to inspire, empower and educate others. However, lets put more than put our two cents in and be a CONSISTENT voice of clarity. What we have to say is worth more than that, don't you think?

2. Some people often talk about good cops taking a stand against bad cops and their need to crack the blue code of silence yet don't offer suggestions how. With any people who are expected to take a stand against injustices, especially when they're in the minority, we must consider their need for a safe-space to do so. In this case a safe-space is a place an officer can fully express themselves without fear of retaliation against them and/or their family or them being made to feel uncomfortable, unwanted or bullied on account of standing against police corruption. If

we expect our officers to have integrity like Frank Serpico then we also need to have their back because some of their partners, an entire precinct and possibly IA (Internal Affairs) may not.

3. Be a constituent, not a voter. The power in the political process is not in itself voting it's in constituency. The difference is one votes with a voice, the other votes with money where their mouth is. On a regional and local level get to know who our officials are and their jurisdictions. Then find out who their constituency is; those who are financially backing them. Then we will see the basis of their policies and expose their political agendas. Even more so we can start identifying or organizing lobbyist groups who are aligned with our agendas and engage these regional and local law makers about what matters to our group, with money, not just our mouth. There's strength in numbers and the numbers in our pocket.

4. Prayer changes things.., when you do something about those "things" after you're done praying. Ever since George W. Bush founded the Faith Based Community Initiative in 2001, churches and other religious organizations have been getting millions of federally funded social service dollars from the U.S. government. One of the reasons you see many of these institutions less likely to get involved with social justice issues, and if they do they're supportive

of the status quo, is because they don't want to bite the hand that's feeding and breeding them. Knowing this, as a congregant you need to hold your leader's feet to the fire and demand that some of your financial support go towards projects, programs, initiatives and collaborations that directly address the racial disparities in your city. If they're unwilling to do anything or their solution is to just pray for your city, you know what time it is.

5. It's a fact we have feelings yet our feelings aren't always a fact. As a matter of fact, our feelings can heal or hurt, build or destroy. We can only make that determination from a conscious place. I know it's challenging, and it may take everything in us to share or not some things, yet we must put thought into what we choose to share. Don't just be angry, articulate that anger. Although I'm sure many of the things I've seen on social media and hear in conversations are well intended. Our children just don't need to pay for our well meaning mistakes.

6. Allies will align themselves with you, don't go begging for them. Keep in mind that white allies must give up a lot in order to systematically fight against racial disparities, police violence and inequalities, not just protest about these issues. Most aren't built like that. How do I know? Because if the majority of the 63% of their U.S. population were built like that we wouldn't be having this discussion

right now. The same white allies were outnumbered during slavery and segregation, that's why the status quo remained the same, that they still got privileges from. They were always grossly outnumbered and some really weren't who they say they were. Also, trying to appeal to a moral conscience of white people, and other people of color, who are not convinced that black lives matter is an exercise in futility. Slaves didn't get free by putting forth some bullet proof argument to convince their masters it was wrong or by making them feel ashamed about their actions. Regardless, we have to be committed enough to do things on our own to protect and support one another.

7. The historical and present day racial disparities, police violence and inequalities against black people in the U.S. and in other colonialist countries don't have any thing to do with race, they have everything to do with race.

Lineage

Our ancestors left clear evidence of their existence, and answers, if we're willing to look, listen and learn.

Successful Resolutions

Reflecting upon any passing year and looking towards the next Gregorian Calendar Year, I just wanted to take a moment to share some of my thoughts with all of you... First and foremost, I want to THANK all of you who invested time in reading my articles, researching the links/information I share via my Facebook Page, checked out and subscribed to my Youtube Channel (A.S.I.A. TV) and Radio Show (Atlantis Build Talk Radio), purchased my literature/music (Quanaah Publishing), and connected with me in whatever capacity we were able to. It is very much appreciated!! The numerous dialogues, testimonials, letters, questions and constructive advice I receive on the daily lets me know that what I do is not in vain. It's serving my intended purpose; encouraging positive growth & development. There are also many people I've had the pleasure of meeting for the first time and others I've had the opportunity to build/rebuild relationships from all over the world. None of us are in each others lives by chance and I look forward to what these bonds continue to positively produce for the future. You are also all very much appreciated!! My Queens are doing very well, I'm very happy about our state of health and there were many things I was able to consistently and successfully accomplish. As far as Resolutions are concerned, I don't have any. I am a work in progress so I'm always exploring ways to improve myself so that I can be a greater resource to others. Living a way of life that includes the phrase 'striving for perfection' as a part of its fundamental principles is the essence of any/all Resolutions. Therefore, I will continue being as resolute as I have been.

For those of you who've made Resolutions, here are 9 Keys that will help you achieve your goals in this upcoming year:

1. Although it is your personal Resolution, your Resolution should be something that improves (progresses) you with the intent/consideration of making you a better resource to others and this World we share. Life is interdependent, we all play a role in how the World turns, and there is a constant process of giving and receiving. This intent/consideration ensures that our Resolution is in tune with the universal order, and is something that is sustainable -because we are actively providing a service that others, and the World, needs. If all we are thinking about is what we can get (keep), and not what we are able to consistently give, what we get (keep) will eventually run out. If you don't believe this, try it with your breath. Keep it to yourself and see how long it takes for your oxygen to run out...

2. Make sure our Resolution is real and obtainable. It's less likely we're going to change EVERYTHING at once, so it's important to work on what we can change, one goal at a time. Also, take things one day at a time.... It took awhile to create habits and it's going to take time to change them. The smaller goals we accomplish serve as stepping stones; helping us build confidence, and gain the tools & experience that are necessary to achieve our larger goals. And with any goal, one of the first and most important steps we need to take, and habits we need to create is to "Get our day underway with a positive, productive attitude." That attitude sets the stage for our altitude.

3. Make your goals specific. Instead of saying something like, "I'm going to read more" say something more specific like, "I am going to read two novels every month." This is called Specificity. This not only helps you better focus on your goals, but it encourages you to be more responsible and committed to your goals. If you were to say, "I want to be healthier this year" there is no sense of ambition or plan of action to achieve that goal. Now if you said, "I am going to only eat baked chicken once a week and go to the gym three times a week for 1 ½ hours" that has a sense of ambition and provides part of a plan of action to achieve your goal of being healthier this year. If it's not clear, your path won't be cleared.

4. Set a projected time/date for your goals. Setting a time/date creates a sense of urgency, responsibility, and accountability to meet your goals. If you don't meet your time/date then set another one. Without setting a time/date then we're saying our goals aren't really a priority (important) -because under these circumstances they can happen any time, and any day. That is not resolute, and if you don't have a time/date, there will probably never be a time/date.

5. Write down your Resolutions. I've known people who had challenges with organizing their day, appropriating their time, and focusing on achieving their goals. One of the solutions I shared with them was writing down their goals on index cards or signs and posting them in visible places around their home. This helped reinforce/remind them of their goals so they wouldn't allow themselves to get lost in the hustle & bustle of the day.

6. Only share your Resolutions with those who have shown themselves to be supportive of you fulfilling them! If they're not there to help you, then they're only going to hinder.

7. Look into networking with people/organizations that will help you fulfill your physical and mental health goals. If you want to cut back on the substances you've been using like drugs/alcohol, or have some mental health issues going on, reach out to any local, regional, national organizations that specifically deal with drug/alcohol abuse and mental health. There are no Resolutions when you don't have your health.

8. Keep a Positive Outlook! Some days it will be easy to maintain a level of positivity and other days you need 'social equality' (fellowship) with others -who share the same goals and are just as resolute as you are about positivity. This means, whatever religious, cultural, or secular organization you are a member of or affiliated with, invest the time to be there and learn as much as you can about the positive principles/values they're sharing with you. This is part of your foundational network and will help you maintain a Positive Outlook when you need the support, which we all do.

9. Your Resolution is not the end all be all. Some people live to have a Wedding while others strive to be Married, have a family, and etc.. While the former is a place, the later is a state. So although your Resolutions may help you arrive at a place, the ultimate goal should be to achieve a state of existence. And this state of existence should set the stage to help us achieve even higher/greater goals! It's all about constant growth and elevation, not stagnation. Life is constantly changing & evolving, and so should the living.

In closing, I will that while reflecting on our past year we consider those negative things we've held fast to that has destroyed our ability to unify with others and undermined our ability to accomplish anything significant on our own. If we think/know we have offended, wronged or hurt somebody, then take advantage of this moment in time to apologize. If you think/know you've been offended, wronged or hurt by somebody, then take advantage of this moment in time to forgive. Begin your New Year with the right mindset, on the right foot and making the right decision to move forward. We've all had challenges within ourselves, and with others, any year, and these lessons learned should empower us to be more positive and progressive in the coming year.

Unity

Men build houses, Women make homes.

Power and Truth

In Truth, sometimes the Power is simple presentation.

Minority Report

Some years ago on March 22nd, 2012 I wrote an article addressing the specific role of people who are classified as white, within our nation. The article was entitled Caucasian Five Percenters. Almost eight years ago on September 8th, 2008 I also shared a video on my Youtube Channel dealing with the same subject matter. You can watch that video "Do Gods and Earths teach Caucasians?" by searching 'Atlantis Build'. I'm referencing them for those of you who never saw them and for those of you who would like to look at them again. It's important, especially nowadays, seeing that this subject has come up again. Due to recent events among the Five Percent I think it's necessary to elaborate on this again, yet from a different perspective. Today I will elaborate more on our specific posture, as original people, when it comes to Caucasians who want to learn our culture.

As Five Percenters we see ourselves as civilized people and as civilized people we are not required to teach/give somebody our cultural curriculum; Supreme Mathematics, the Supreme Alphabet or 120 lessons. According to our lessons, civilize means to teach knowledge and wisdom of all the human families of the planet earth. Our lessons also confirm that civilization is one having knowledge, wisdom, understanding, culture, refinement and is not a savage in the pursuit of happiness. We further learn that the duty of a civilized person is to teach he [of her] who is savage civilization, righteousness, the knowledge of himself, the science of everything in life, love, peace and happiness. None of these lessons say or even imply that we must give somebody Supreme Mathematics, the Supreme Alphabet or 120 lessons. In my early years of having KOS [Knowledge Of Self] I didn't understand this and anyone who seemed halfway interested in my culture I would start formally teaching them Supreme Mathematics, the Supreme Alphabet or 120 lessons. The result of that was people sifting through all of the time and teachings I shared with them to simply preserve what they considered to be the best part for themselves. All of them learned Supreme Mathematics, the Supreme Alphabet or 120 lessons to some degree. When it came down to application, some only went as far as no longer eating pork meat. Others legally changed their name and/or gave their children righteous names. Some literally moved to Jerusalem to live off of the grid and many others became successful leaders in their respective industries and credit it to what they learned through me. If I would have been wise enough to properly assess what resonated with them the most upfront, I could have saved time and resources by simply teaching them that. Nowadays I'm not so quick to just formally give somebody Supreme Mathematics, the Supreme Alphabet or 120 lessons. I know that if more of us took that responsible approach today we wouldn't see the degree of inconsistency, insincerity, disloyalty, inactivity and outright ignorance in our nation.

In the past I've noted that people reached out to me to from around the world in order to learn more about my culture and many of them were Caucasian. That was 4 years ago and even more people reach out to me now. From what I've seen among some of the Five Percent is they haven't been taught how to handle this situation when they want to learn. Some simply say we teach all the human families of the planet earth, use Azreal as a template, and give them everything. Others say we cannot reform the devil and wouldn't touch a white person with a ten-foot pole. Neither usually offers practical procedures or a basic "how to" handle it when the situation arises. Oftentimes you hear name calling and rhetorical jargon to cosign what someone personally wants to do.

Musa's hard time

Let me again reiterate that we are civilized people. As a civilized person, the most just position we can take in regards to anybody learning, including Caucasians, is that everyone has the opportunity to be civilized. Whether they'll do what is necessary to be civilized and advocate civilization, that is entirely up to them, not us. If they don't follow through we cannot be in a position to be blamed for it. That would be wrong and according to our lessons we are all wise, righteous, just and true. If they don't follow through it must be because they denied themselves, not because we denied them by saying they ain't got what it takes, they're weak or etc. To say what somebody will/won't be able to do puts us in a position to possibly be proven wrong -and some people live to prove others wrong, right? Right. If we consider ourselves just or a standard of justice, this also puts our sense of justice in a position to possibly be proven flawed. It's like a plumber talking about how perfect their work was in stopping a leak, but then water finds a way to seep through. What does that say about their work and the materials they used to complete it? The wisest posture we can have towards anyone is that they have a chance to clean themselves up. Again, this chance doesn't mean we're required to teach/give somebody Supreme Mathematics, the Supreme Alphabet or 120 lessons. This means that we must be a source of knowledge, wisdom, understanding, culture, refinement and not a savage in the pursuit of happiness. By saying "everyone has a chance", we cannot be blamed for any of their shortcomings. If we were to say "you have no chance" and a person some how pulls off the impossible, we look like an ass and our standard of judgement does too.

Our 9th degree in the 1-14's is specifically there to represent this chance. It highlights a blameless posture and reiterates that our sense of justice is flawless. This is why is proceeds the 10th degree which declares a person is 100% incorrigible. You cannot proclaim somebody 100% weak, wicked and lawless without first giving them a chance to have access to the law. Then and only then can we say they didn't obey. That is justice and in the 9th degree that justice is symbolic to a sword. One of the things I often share with other Five Percenters is this: the same sword we may hold over someone's head in order to correct them is actually in our hand. Therefore, we must hold ourselves to a much higher standard of righteousness and civilization than what we expect from others; it's literally in our hands. Again, I am not talking about giving somebody Supreme Mathematics, the Supreme Alphabet or 120 lessons. I'm talking about the proper attitude and posture of a civilized person and how we need to treat anybody.

Let's get into some other things that I want to clarify about Caucasians striving to learn our culture. One of the issues that come up is their names. First and foremost, original people within our nation choose righteous names because most of our original names, language, customs and traditions were taken from us via the Trans-Atlantic Slave Trade and Colonialism. This arrested our cultural development and disconnected us from our identity and ancestral legacy. This didn't happen to Caucasians. Because many of our people do not know the original language or names our ancestors used we choose righteous names to reconnect with the principles and values that denotes our true identity as the Fathers and Mothers of civilization. It's not necessary for a Caucasian woman who is of Irish descent to change her name from Aileen Murphy; that's Irish and a part of her uninterrupted ancestry. It's also not necessary for a Caucasian man of Italian descent to call himself anything other than his Italian birth name Alessio Dinapoli; his family is from Naples. Even when the scenario is a Caucasian person who considers themselves American, yet they're primarily a hodgepodge of European ancestry; their birth name is still going to represent part of that uninterrupted German, French, Dutch or etc. lineage. It's their job to bring honor to their birth name and be a righteous example to their family, community and people as a whole. Now some would argue that the Father gave Azreal a righteous name and that is not true. Azreal is not one of our names. Let me also share this, whenever a Five Percenter meets another Five Percenter there are 3 primary questions that's asked: 1.) What's your name? 2.) What degrees [lessons] are you dealing with and how long have you had KOS [Knowledge Of Self]? and 3.) Who is your educator? In regards to names, it's not uncommon to meet someone with one that isn't right and exact or a name they cannot show and prove. When this occurs the person is corrected and told to choose something different. Examples of this is a dude with the name Equality, a 50/50 dude in prison claiming he's half Blood and half Five Percent with the name Murder Allah or a Caucasian woman with Divine in her name. Whenever a person is addressed about this, especially by our elders, and they still refuse to make the necessary changes, that bold defiance is viewed as a sign of disrespect, contempt and the unwillingness to adhere to our cultural standards. Back in the day people got their ass whopped for that. Nowadays people usually get bombed [chastised] and banned from attending any local, regional and national events because they're not listening or striving to learn anyway.

In regards to regalia, original women, who represent the Earth within our nation, cover 3/4th's of their body and customarily wear head wraps [crowns]. As the Earth is covered 3/4th's under water, 139,685,000 square miles of water and 57,255,000 square miles of land, our women dress modestly. Also, in many tropical/equatorial countries the head wrap was used to protect our woman's head from the sun rays. We consider all of this her refinement because that style of dress reflects the cultural elegance, sophistication, grace and status of a Queen. Caucasian women who are striving to learn about our culture should also dress modesty, yet not as our Queens or the Earth because she's not them. The same can be said about Caucasian men; they shouldn't be wearing our crowns, especially with "Allah" on it, because they are not the true and living God. Anyone on the outside looking in should not be confused about what they're looking at and never mistake a Caucasian for a God or Earth.

In closing, keep in mind that Five Percenters are not a Rainbow Coalition nor are we Black Militants. We are critical thinkers and have an allegiance to the truth, regardless where it comes from. Those of us who are educators, who know our cultural curriculum, "informally" teach that truth to anyone yet choose who we want to "formally" teach. Informal education is like general civilization; people learn just simply observing or being in proximity to us. Formal education is like training units; people directly learn more specifically about our culture and how we live. Whether it's general civilization or training units that still does not require us to give somebody Supreme Mathematics, the Supreme Alphabet or 120 lessons. Training can be any form of basic instruction, guidance or exercises we use to inspire, empower and educate people to be more civilized. Our cultural curriculum is sacred and should never be handed out to people like welfare cheese or we're on the block hittin' licks. I encourage those of you who are coming in contact with Caucasians who are interested in learning to refer to my article Caucasian Five Percenters. It gives you further insight on how to approach that situation and what to expect from Caucasians. You're not obligated to give them Supreme Mathematics, the Supreme Alphabet or 120 lessons but you are obligated to treat them civilized and share with them any general civilization and/or training units they can use to help clean themselves up to be a better resource within their home, community, among their own people, to original people and to the planet earth. Their men and women cannot be Gods or Earths because God and the Earth was already here and accounted for before they got here. They're not Kings or Queens 'within' our nation because that is not their birth right, role or title here. As the Fathers and Mothers of civilization we were the rulers and established this righteous monarchy before they got here. When it comes to their own household and community it's important that they govern those domains with righteous authority and be royal standards among their own people. The bottom line is Caucasians who come among us can learn to do like us yet cannot be us.

Priorities

I don't subscribe to the idea of excuses, I'm all about prioritizing. Whatever we see as important, we will find a way to get it done. Even when there are extenuating circumstances or inclement weather; when that subsides we will still get it done! People will tell you they didn't read five pages of a book today yet they did read five Facebook or Instagram pages they're stalking. They'll say they couldn't get up early to workout yet they got up and out early to hit Tim Hortons and get to work. Most times, whatever we are or aren't doing comes down to our priorities.

120 Lessons
Role Playing Games and Elevation

Back in the day one of my favorite role-playing games [RPGs] for the NES [Nintendo Entertainment System] was called Rygar. Visually it's nothing in comparison to today's computer graphics but the story line, difficulty level and graphics were golden when in dropped in '86. I was eleven at the time. Rygar was a warrior who came back from the dead to defeat an evil being who had taken over the peaceful land of Argool. In his quest Rygar uses a fiery shield and other weapons to accomplish this task of restoring peace throughout the land. Also, important clues are given to him by large sage-like men that he meets in green stone temples throughout the game. To complete each stage Rygar had to defeat a God and the final God he fought in his castle in the sky. One of the complexities of this game is the fact that it did not save and when the game ended; you had to start from the beginning. Playing this game wasn't easy and everybody didn't mess with Rygar.

When I first got KOS [Knowledge Of Self] through learning to recite and study 120 lessons I couldn't help but recognize the parallels between my degrees and role-playing video games like Rygar. Like Rygar, we as scientists of life, are the lessons central figure who's striving to complete a series of quests to reach the conclusion of its central storyline; national consciousness, community control and peace. Our Argool is the planet Earth. Along our quest there are also various people places and things we encounter and learn life lessons from. In 120 there are approximately 100 characters (Doctor, Little Boy, Musa, Mother and etc.) 60 geographic locations (India, West Asia, Africa, North America and etc.) and 40 objects (Coat, Gold, Steel, Shield and etc.). Like with all role-playing video games such as Rygar, exploring different realms is vital to its game play. In 120 that realm or world is 196,940,000 square miles; 57,255,000 sq. miles of land, 139,685,000 sq. miles of water and 790,613,581,824,000,000 sq. inches in total. We also learn that this world is one among other planets, in a solar system, in proximity to the Sun. While some were approaching these degrees as just information to memorize, I began to realize that these degrees were stages teaching me how to navigate life. If you failed a stage in Rygar you had to return to the beginning. If you didn't know a degree in 120 you have to go back to the beginning of that degree, or possibly all of your lessons, to get it right and exact.

The irony of this is that there are those who claim to be Five Percenters, and those seeking to learn this culture, who treat this way of life like it's a game. They're not serious about civilization, righteousness or the knowledge of themselves; they're playing. They don't know 120 or aren't striving to learn our degrees -which is 6/8th's or 75% of what we learn about the culture. Although this is customary among Five Percenters, if you ask "them" questions about our lessons they get offended or start ducking and dodging you like a bill collector or the repo man.

100% of the Map

Another very important aspect of 120 that I strive to communicate is that it's a map. This map highlights the chronology, nomenclature, cultural landmarks, events, people, places and things from the perspective of the original people. While we are currently in 2016 according to the Christian Calendar, as Five Percenters we recognize this year as 15,102 according the Asiatic Calendar. While most celebrate January 1st at midnight as the New Year, we recognize the Spring Equinox at sunrise as the New Year. While there are certain cultural landmarks, events, people, places and things we recognize in common, they're from a different vantage point of view. For example, if we're talking about the founding of this country, while some whites and people of color identify with America's forefathers Declaration of Independence, we see it as colonization and some of our ancestors government sanctioned enslavement even though some of us were enslaved here for 221 years prior to 1776. It's an entirely different perspective of the world, what is or isn't significant to us and how we as first world people relate to the other members of the human family and the planet earth. In one of our lessons we learn about the purpose and establishment of Freemasonry and Shrinedom. While there is a general customer service explanation of its origins in Europe in 1717 we learn that it started with us at a much earlier date when we taught Caucasians how to build homes for themselves and live a respectful life. In regards to nomenclature, there are certain words and phrases we don't use among ourselves that are fine to use in another society. Instead of using "try" we use "strive" because try simply means to fail. While others simply speak of "time" we call it "true I master equality." Learning 120 is a rewiring of our brains which creates a new psychological orientation to think differently about ourselves and what we've been taught about life -especially from the youngest members of the human family, not the fathers and mothers of civilization. It's a psychological orientation that equips us with the proper knowledge, wisdom and understanding to become culturally free and empowered to live a life of peace and harmony. By default, this perspective dismantles the concept of white supremacy, racism, sexism and other maladaptive ideals. I talk about this journey in more detail on Episode 3 of Atlantis Build Talk Radio "The Three Fold Path."

In closing, I cannot stress enough that 120 is 6/8th's or 75% of what we learn about the culture. If this were reflected in the above map it would represent the majority of it. Imagine striving to navigate that map with only 12.5% [Supreme Mathematics] or even 25% [Supreme Mathematics and Supreme Alphabet] of it. This means that the majority of the chronology, nomenclature, cultural landmarks, events, people, places and things from the perspective of the original people would be missing. It would look exactly like below; the same map as above yet the white highlights all that a person is missing.

25% of the Map

This is one of the reasons there are people who claim to be Five Percenters who demonstrate a contradictory lifestyle; they don't have 120 and they're filling in the blanks and making up stuff as they go, especially those without an Enlightener [navigator]. Because some people don't know their degrees there's a chronology of our people, nomenclature, cultural landmarks, events, people, places and things they do not see on this map. Will they come across some things? Yes, given the proper attitude, aptitude and altitude yet it's still guesswork and literally searching for something that doesn't exist. This is also what makes a person easily led... Does this mean that just because someone has the map that they're all good? Hecks naw! Even if someone knows the map they still need to make wise navigational decisions and understand it culturally. There are those who may know 120 forwards and backwards yet still aren't doing what's necessary to advance to higher stages of life. All in all, if you're striving to learn and live out the culture of the Five Percent you need to learn 120 along with Supreme Mathematics and Supreme Alphabet. Don't stagnate, elevate.

Lauryn Hilliotheraphy

For those of you who've been keeping up with Lauryn Hill's career, over the last couple of years she's resurfaced and has begun to perform again. Sometime after dropping her critically acclaimed solo album the Miseducation of Lauryn Hill she virtually disappeared from public life and became a recluse; not performing, recording or conducting any interviews. In a Tumblr post around 2012 L-Boogie stated that she had withdrawn from society to protect her family's safety amid a "climate of hostility, false entitlement, manipulation, racial prejudice, sexism and ageism." Although her catalog and accomplishments are not many, she is peerless when it comes to the impact of her presence and the quality of her creative contributions. One of the concerns she has publicly voiced on various occasions, that many of us have seen voiced by others such as Nina Simone, is the cultural contradiction that has come along with her making those contributions within the context of this society and Capitalistic economy. As she's done in the past when her eccentric behavior had people speculating mental health issues, Lauryn Hill has recently demonstrated some consistent challenges making her performances on time. In regards to one of her most recent performances in Atlanta Georgia where she was over two hours late, she has this to say, in part, about the great deal of criticism she's received, "*I don't show up late to shows because I don't care. And I have nothing but Love and respect for my fans. The challenge is aligning my energy with the time, taking something that isn't easily classified or contained, and trying to make it available for others. I don't have an on/off switch. I am at my best when I am open, rested, sensitive and liberated to express myself as truthfully as possible.*"

In any creative artist's defense, I think it's important to understand that in parts of the East, what Lauryn Hill is striving to communicate about aligning her "*energy with the time, taking something that isn't easily classified or contained, and trying to make it available for others*" and "*accommodate the vitality, spontaneity, and spirit that make the performances*" is commonly understood. In parts of the East artists play when and if they feel like it, for however long they desire, and their listeners understand the essence of that creativity. If an artist is scheduled to play, say at sundown,

and they decide not to play or come hours later, the people aren't upset or critical of them. One such artist was Hazrat Inayat Khan; a renown veena player, author and founder of the Sufi Order in the West. Even within an orchestra, conductors in the East are musicians that play along with the other musicians in the orchestra. In the West, conductors are separate from their orchestra. Again, this exists in parts of the East, particularly among those who have held fast to traditions prior to colonialism and their influence from the western world. Here in the West we also see this Eastern influence prevalent within post 1945 improvisation Jazz music and the freestyle/creative dance, fashion, graffiti, deejay and rap elements within Hip Hop culture.

Now, if you are an actual performing artist such as Lauryn Hill, doing business within this or any country, signing contracts and making money from those performances, publishing rights and intellectual property, you are legally obligated. You are obligated to meet deadlines and be punctual because it's part of your financial lifeline. You're working on yours and others time. You, and those who you are doing business with, are required to contractually keep their word as bond because this economy is not based upon an honor system. There is no way around that in regards to business. Just as I am sure Lauryn Hill has some financial expectations from those whom she does business with for her family, those who do business with her have expectations too -like the record contract she did in 2013 with Sony that helped cover her tax debt. The closest one in modern times to what Lauryn Hill is striving to articulate about one's ability to "accommodate the vitality, spontaneity, and spirit that make the performances" was ODB [Ol Dirty Bastard]. He pretty much did whatever he wanted; showed up when he wanted, came late, left early, didn't do photo shoots or interviews that were scheduled, broke out of rehab and showed up at concerts to perform, didn't finish songs, interrupted the Grammy's, took MTV to the county office in a limo to pick up his welfare check, wore one shoe on an Arsenio Hall show performance, used his benefit card for his album cover and a host of other things. L-Boogie is not ODB.

Lauryn Hill, regardless if you'd like to call her a creative, performing artist or musician, is working within the context of a western society based upon Capitalism and governed by the business rules & regulations she enters into via contractual agreements. As for Lauryn Hill, if she is being paid by people to do something then she needs to do it. If there's a legitimate reason why she's not able to fulfill that obligation, like Beyonce had to reschedule her Nashville concert due to stadium construction, then Lauryn Hill needs to professionally address that. It's not that sophisticated, complicated or philosophical. It's fickle, temperamental and perhaps arrogant or Narcissistic to expect people to unquestionably do things for us yet expect them to "be understandable" if/when we consistently don't do things to reciprocate that. In any arena of life with relationships, whether its business, platonic, romantic or etc., it's important to have a sense of equality. It's unfair to expect otherwise. If Lauryn Hill chooses to continue performing and make music to financially support her family she has two options which should also include more speaking engagements to educate her audience. I emphasize the educational component because many Westerners, and even Easterners influenced by the West, have no clue what she often talks about in regards to cultural creative freedom. Many of us creative artists do. So her two options are: 1.) Figure out an effective way to equally honor her creativity and her contractual agreements. 2.) Disconnect from the entertainment industry and strive to make a living by further exploring some of the Eastern approaches towards artistic expression that I spoke of. Willfully she gets it together because the world needs more of what she has offered.

Asiyah Finah and Aziza Fari

I'll tell you, what makes me prouder than anything in this world, more than any of my personal accomplishments, is seeing my young Queens actively involved in initiatives and sharing commentary on cultural, socioeconomic and race issues to enlighten the people.

Conversations

HIM: I don't believe in God.

ME: Huh?

HIM: I don't believe in God, I call him "He who has created

all things."

ME: So... what do...

HIM: [cutting me off] And doooon't try to convince me otherwise. Lol

ME: Naw, I was wondering what you say when you're having amazing sex since you don't say, "Oh. My. God!"

HIM: Awww man, you crazy! Lol

ME: I'm serious, when your eyes roll in the back of your head what do you say, "Oh My.. He Who Has Created All Things"?

HIM: LOL!!

The Jaguar

Some of us men love to be the lion out in the open plains. They roar, got a mane, sleep a lot, yet allow the lioness' to do the hunting but are always the first to eat. If and when they do kill, like most other big cats, lions hold their prey by the throat and suffocate them to death.

Although I appreciate some of the attributes of a lion, I prefer to be a jaguar, particularly a black one. They're stealth and move in silence. They live in the midst of the jungle, don't roll in a pride and have the strongest bite pound for pound. Unlike any of the other big cats, jaguars don't suffocate their prey. Jaguars kill their prey swiftly by biting them in the skull. That's more reflective of how I move.

Our ancestors and present day descendants have always gained insight through our observation of nature. This wisdom was/is especially made born through identifying the attributes of animals; often illustrated as zoomorphic forms.

An Atrophy of Elevation

I'm sorry but some of us act like we got an online degree in Hidden Colorology. We just stopped going to church last Easter, we don't have one book a decade old but we're on social media trying to bang on people like Rowdy Roddy Piper in Piper's Pit? Not only is it immature but it shows that we're really no different than that fire & brimstone storefront preacher at St. Luke Morningstar Meadow Redemption Tabernacle of the Living God in Christ Church we despise. Trying to ridicule, clown, belittle, scare, bully or embarrass people into accepting what we believe is true isn't the truth. The truth doesn't need to do all that, just like the Sun ain't trying to convince a bunch of people that it shines.

Are We Eating Our Young?

People often don't realize how much of an impact the economy really has on us psychologically and socially. If you let the tell-lie-vision tell it, we're not in an Economic Recession right now and everything is good on main street in America. How? Because measuring economic decline is accompanied by a visible stock market drop, a decline in the housing market and increase in unemployment. Those factors, along with a decline in the gross domestic product (GDP) for a couple of consecutive quarters, are the standards of measurement used by the dominant mainstream society.

Those standards can fool a person into believing that everything is alright. Where many of us live around the world, whenever we've been in proximity to global white supremacy and institutionalized racism/sexism, our communities have been in more than a Recession, it's an Economic Suppression. Historically speaking and with very few exceptions, whenever main street America has a cold, the back streets and country roads will have the bird flu. Today I'm not going to just talk about the economy's impact on us, I'm going to talk about how our psychology and sociology, via mythology, shapes the economy. I'm also going to talk about the vital role of fathers in leading our families and communities.

The image above of Cronus is Greek and the Greeks are considered the hallmark and standard of so-called Western Civilization. When you study their mythos, two of the most common themes you'll find is a preoccupation with time [Chronophobia] and Infanticide [life and death]. Cronus was the son of Uranus, no pun intended. Uranus had sex with his wife Gaia [Earth] every night but hated the children she bore him; the Titans. So what did Uranus do? He imprisoned them in a place called Tartarus which is equivalent to Hell. This caused Gaia great pain so she did what any scorned woman would do: she shaped a great flint-bladed sickle and asked her children to cut Uranus' penis off. The only one brave enough to do it was their youngest child, Cronus, so when he caught his Father out there he castrated him. The blood that spilled from Uranus onto Gaia gave birth to the Hekatonkheires [the three 100 handed giants], the one-eyed giants called the Cyclopes, Erinyes [female punisher deities], Meliae [tree 'nymphs'; where nymphomaniac is derived] and the deity Aphrodite was born from Uranus' severed balls [testicles] that Cronus threw in the sea. After all of this Cronus re-imprisoned his brothers the Hekatonkheires and Cyclopes in Tartarus, and he too faced the same fate of being overthrown by his future son Zeus. Because Cronus was aware of this self-fulfilled prophesy he tried to defy fate by eating his own children. The above image is of Cronus eating one of his children. Eventually his wife Rhea tricked him by wrapping a stone in a blanket and hiding their child Zeus who was raised away from his Father Cronus and grew up to one day over take him. When Zeus came of age he first caused his Father to throw up his siblings whom he ate. Then Zeus freed his uncles the Hekatonkheires and Cyclopes from Tartarus and they along with his siblings defeated Cronus in the battle know as the Titanomachy. Oh yeah, to thank Zeus for releasing them his uncles the Cyclopes gave him thunder and lightening.

This is just a small glimpse of the dysfunction found throughout Greek Mythology; the psychological and sociological backdrop to Roman Mythology, a segment of

Europe and the good ole U.S. of A. I focused on the Father-Son relationships of Uranus, Cronus and Zeus because it highlights some the trans-generational daddy issues we see prevalent throughout American society. Uranus didn't want to yield to Chronus and Chronus didn't want to yield to Zeus. Living in a society where we often see this resentment that the old heads sometimes carry for the young bucks, and the young bucks likewise carry for old heads, has created a generational gap that mirrors the same conditions that perpetuated the dysfunction throughout Greek Mythology. When the Baby Boomers and Generation X are not preparing a place of leadership for the Millennials, our families, communities and society suffers. When the Millennials are not seeking guidance from the Baby Boomers and Generation X, our families, communities and society suffers too. It's a lose-lose situation and this has become an issue on main street, the back streets and the country roads in America.

When there's an Economic Recession and Economic Suppression, this further compounds these issues. When this is not taken into consideration sometimes people believe the old suppress the young; older people stay in positions stopping the children from having opportunities because they're jealous, haters or simply set in their ways. That's not always the case where there's an Economic Recession and Economic Suppression going on. Sometimes it's just good old fashioned fear. Fear of not having enough money to live on or to pay for medical bills that come with waning health/vitality. Fear of social security, pensions, 401K and etc. drying up or being taken away. This whole idea of a vanishing middle class and an expanding American landscape of haves and havenots is real. Many of the people you see working every day who are over 65 are not doing it as a hobby or for pocket money; they're supplementing a fixed income. Consider this the next time you hear people say career politicians, doorstop pastors and Adamantium labor/trade unions are just hating on the youth. Yes, some absolutely are and don't care about what happens to our youth or the future of this society. Some are just striving to hold on to a financial lifeline Congress is slowly cutting away. On the flip size, all of our youth aren't just rebels without a cause, unruly or anti-elders. Many of them are dissatisfied with the present conditions and want to change things yet may not know what to do or where to even start. They're in an Economic Recession and Economic Suppression too. Many of the people you see not working every day who are young are not doing it because they're lazy or would rather beg for pocket money; they don't know how, where, when or what to do to supplement their family's fixed income.

There's a terrible disparity between fathers and suns in our communities that must be reconciled. Some fathers simply don't desire to have a relationship with their suns. Like

59

Uranus, he may have enjoyed the sex with a female [Gaia] every night but hate the sun(s) she bore him. Sometimes there are females standing between a father and sun who are not striving to or even qualified to help them reconcile that relationship. Like Gaia, she may have experienced great pain from her relationship with the father and eventually created an environment for their sun(s) to cut him off [castrate him]. These Grecian narratives have become a common psychology and social backdrop within our communities that continues to erode our family units and local living economies. If fathers aren't passing on the insight, guidance and skillsets to their suns it arrests their child's development and limits their ability to make a living for themselves and contribute to this society. As a youth advocate there have been many young males I've mentored who were in this position. I've done and continue to do my part by providing them with the resources to successfully make that transition into manhood. As this Greek Mythology of Chronophobia and Infanticide was passed on through its generations it requires a paradigm shift on our part to redefine our family units and communities. This requires more than research on alternatives, it requires application. In the most simplistic terms we as men need to father our suns. If we don't have a sun we need to be father figures. How? By being a link to their future by nurturing, respecting, loving, protecting and educating them. The women who our suns were born through, or who are mother figures, must help reconcile that father-sun relationship and not stand in the way.

Senate Bill No. 227

In regards to grand jury indictments, "Senate Bill No. 227" is the legislation that was passed in California [August 2015] banning secret grand juries from inquiring into cases involving excessive/deadly force or misconduct by law enforcement that led to the death of a person being detained or arrested. Lobbyist pressure needs to be put upon other State Legislatures to adopt the same legislation. This is another approach we can use to address the non indictments we've seen and the criminal justice system's reluctance to hold its law enforcement accountable for their actions.

Cultural Context

In the early 1960's while a black man known as The Father [Allah] started a movement called The Five Percenters; teaching young adults self actualization on the East Coast [New York] who took on names like Divine, Master, Al Jamel, Wisdom, Moon and etc. with the family name Allah, a white man known as Father [Yod] started a movement called The Source Family; teaching young adults self actualization on the

West Coast [California] who took on names like Electricity, Ah-Om, Heaven, Yahowa #3, Galaxy, Harvest Moon and etc. with the family name Aquarian.

That Priceless Look of Poverty

Regardless how well intended and proficient doctors may be, they are in the sick business. If they healed patients, we would rarely need doctors so they "treat" them instead -and the pharmaceutical companies aren't mad about it. The same can be said about lawyers; they are in the crime, personal injury and family dysfunction business. If it weren't for drugs, violence, accidents, divorces and etc., we would rarely need them too. I'm sure my barber is glad indestructible haircuts don't exist yet because he would be out of business too. Whether we are mechanics, school teachers, dentists, politicians, pastors or etc., there's a certain degree of job security that comes along with fixing things or even striving to insure that things remain broke, as in "poor."

Divine Science

God is the nature & apex of the Black Man! The only standard worthy of being our model of self actualization.

Filibusters
#SCOTUS Obstructionists of Justice

Filibuster: *an action such as a prolonged speech that obstructs progress in a legislative assembly while not technically violating the required procedures. To act in an obstructive manner in a legislature, especially by speaking at inordinate length.*

A couple of colleagues {Akeem Rashad Allah/DJ Wise and Salim Adofo} and I had the privilege to be on a conference call directly from the White House with other key African American and Civil Rights Leaders around the country about the Supreme Court nomination process that was moderated by Stephanie Young and Valerie Jarrett. Stephanie Young is the Director of African American Outreach for The White

House and Valerie Jarrett is the Senior Adviser to President Barack Obama and Assistant for Public Engagement and Intergovernmental Affairs in his Administration. If you're unfamiliar with these women I encourage you to Google them. Also read President Obama's "A Responsibility I Take Seriously" statement.

Following the death of Supreme Court Justice and ultra-conservative Antonin Scalia, this left a vacancy in the highest court of our country. According to our Constitution, in order to fill that vacancy the current President, in our case President Barack Obama, chooses a nominee who is then confirmed by the Senate and then appointed to that position. This is a process that requires several steps, which on average has taken 67 days since 1975, roughly two months, and every U.S. Supreme Court nominee in history has received a vote within four months. President Obama has over 300 days left to serve his second term as our commander and chief so there shouldn't be a problem nominating another Supreme Court Justice, unless of course the Senate doesn't cooperate. After our President makes his nomination it's then sent to the Senate Judiciary Committee who conducts hearings to question his nomination to determine if they'll make a suitable Supreme Court Justice. When these hearings conclude, the Judiciary Committee votes on whether the President's nomination should go to the full Senate with a good, bad or neutral report. Republicans in the Judiciary Committee, led by their chairman Sen. Charles Grassley of Iowa, have already made it publicly known that they are not going to vote for whoever our President nominates. The last time a Supreme Court nominee was denied a hearing was in 1875. To give you some context, this was 141 years ago during the Reconstruction Era when the Civil Rights Act of 1875 was passed to guarantee African Americans access to equal housing, transportation and jury duty inclusion. By delaying this nomination process and dragging their feet, these Republicans and their special-interest group supporters, could very well get their way and there are no formal repercussions by doing this. The only repercussions they face are from their constituents. So instead of upholding the Constitution and doing the job they were elected to do, they have chosen to be filibusters. The bottom line is "they" want "their people" in that position and will do whatever they can to block, obstruct and go against the Constitution and what President Obama was elected to do in serving his final term as our commander and chief. These tactics aren't new and reflect the continuous uphill battle our President and First Lady have dealt with the entire two terms they've been in office. A battle with elected officials being uncooperative, unhelpful, unsupportive and outright disrespectful.

Most say Senate should hold hearings and vote on Obama's nominee to replace Justice Scalia

The Senate should ...

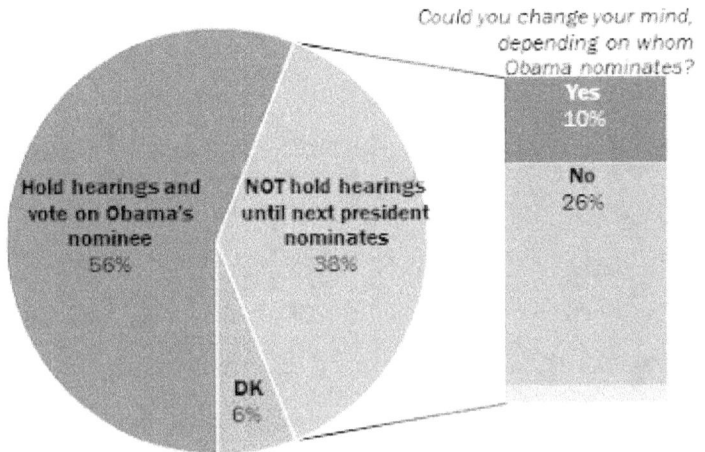

Could you change your mind, depending on whom Obama nominates?

Yes 10%

No 26%

Hold hearings and vote on Obama's nominee 56%

NOT hold hearings until next president nominates 38%

DK 6%

Source: Survey conducted Feb. 18-21, 2016.
Figures may not add to 100% because of rounding.

PEW RESEARCH CENTER

Members of the Republican controlled Senate and Judiciary Committee have tried to argue that the 2016 President-Elect, not our current President, should nominate a Supreme Court Justice because it's an election year. Mind you, the Senate has confirmed 6 Justices in presidential election years since 1900 including the Republican President Ronald Reagan who appointed Justice Kennedy. If the Senate fails to act, the Supreme Court could have a vacancy for the better part of two Terms. This means that without a 9th Justice, the Supreme Court's 4-4 decisions can't legally establish uniform, nationwide rules. Many have been outraged at the sense of defiance, recklessness and disrespect on the part of the Senate Judiciary Committee and according to the Leadership Conference on Civil and Human Rights & The Leadership Conference Education Fund, "*a broad coalition of 82 civil rights, voting rights, public interest, environmental, labor, religious, and education groups sent a letter to Senate Judiciary Chairman Charles Grassley (R-Iowa) and the 10 other Republican members of the Senate Judiciary Committee, condemning their recent announcement that they will refuse to hold a hearing on—or even meet with—any potential Supreme Court nominee.*"

Because there are no formal repercussions the Senate Judiciary Committee will face, except from their constituents, what did we do and what can you do under similar circumstances to create political pressure? First I encouraged people to share my article about this via their social networks including the hash tags #SCOTUS and #DoYourJob. These five points are also actions I took and encouraged others to take in order to amplify this message:

1. Post/Share media interviews, memes, articles and statements via your social networks that talk about the importance of the President's constitutional duty to ensure we have a full supreme court.

2. Post/Share media interviews, memes, articles and statements via your social networks that talk about the role of the court, the role of the President and/or the role of Congress when a seat on the Court needs filling.

3. Post/Share media interviews, memes, articles and statements in the comment section of media interviews, memes, articles and statements via your social networks.

4. Be sure to include the hash tags #SCOTUS and #DoYourJob in all of your postings and commentary.

5. Find out the position of your regional and local public officials on this Supreme Court nomination where you live. Require them to state this position publicly and hold them to it as a matter of their policy record -regardless if they're running for reelection this year or in the future.

Keep in mind that this filibuster scenario that's playing out on the national stage is also happening on a regional and local level throughout America. The reason you may not see certain things getting done in your municipality, your neighborhood or in your workplace is because of the same kind of people striving to block, obstruct and go against progress. Letting our voice be heard about the Supreme Court nomination informs the Senate Judiciary Committee that we will individually/collectively use our position, finances and vote to ensure that people like them, who are not doing their job, will not be in these positions to obstruct justice. We are also informing their constituents that we will not support them, especially in business. How can you trust a business person to do the right thing for their patrons [citizens] when they're deliberately supporting public servants who are not willing to do the right thing for their tax paying citizenry? All of us as citizens are expected to do our job and the citizens we've elected as public servants need to do their jobs too. It's just that simple.

Jul 08, 2016 3:25pm

I had a discussion with the students in my STYA Summer Enrichment Program yesterday about the police violence and deaths of Alton Sterling & Philando Castile. Told them to look it up and research it for themselves. They came back today with some very insightful perspectives on that and updates on the deaths of the police officers in Dallas, TX. Their consensus was it's "The Purge: Election Year."

Beyoncé
The Duchess of Viralshire

When Beyoncé broke the internet Super Bowl week with the release of her Formation video, 2016 Super Bowl Halftime Performance and Take My Hand, Precious Lord mini-documentary, two things primarily happened; people reacted and people responded. From Political Talking Heads, Barbershop Talk, 15 second Instagram Vloggers, Conspiracy Theorists, Conservatives and Entertainment Bloggers, everybody and they Momma had something to say, positively and negatively. On February 9th, one of my colleagues Salim

Adofo, Vice-Chair of the NBUF [National Black United Front], shared this poignant thought via his Facebook Page which effectively summarizes the same perspective I share:

"You can have whatever critique of Beyoncé that you want to have. The fact is she has help to keep the conversation of Black Resistance alive and in the mainstream media for the time being. I see this as a teachable moment. I understand the power and influence a mega star like Beyoncé has and if an incorrect message is sent out, it could be very misleading. Beyoncé is going to do what she is going to do. I cannot control that. However what I can control are the elements of my own cipher. I just need to perform my duty as a civilized man and continue to teach freedom, justice and equality. This gives me another avenue to educate some one that I may have not been able to reach before."

On a personal level, I like Beyoncé's business acumen, work ethic and of course her beauty and sex appeal. Above all, I enjoy seeing how she communicates the complex dimensions of a woman; it's a level of sophistication you oftentimes don't see. Many women, especially in mainstream entertainment, are one maybe two-dimensional. If they ooze sexuality, that's all you see and it may take them a lifetime to change that perception. If they're chronically single and about that turn-up lifestyle, they may never successfully transition into a wife or mother, even if they got married and had a child. Beyoncé is an archetype of a woman's multi-facets. She's able to successfully and seamlessly articulate a variety of a woman's dimensions, which are, yet definitely not limited to, a Mother, Diva, Daughter, Sister, Wife, Bonnie [partner of Clyde] Queen, Girlfriend, Round The Way Girl, Sexy/Erotic, Activist and etc. Beyoncé's most recent manifestation is the real Sasha Fierce; the archetypal Phoenix from the X-Men, Dr. Jean Grey's alter-ego and one of the most powerful mutants. If you understand the context in which Stan Lee created the X-Men, the correspondence of Professor X. to Martin Luther King Jr. and Magneto to Malcolm X., what I'm saying makes perfect sense. In my assessment, some of the women who don't like Beyoncé oftentimes dislike one of her dimensions. Sometimes it's the same dimension they have yet to manifest. In other words, some women who criticize Beyoncé about her sex appeal, don't have sex appeal. Not all women are like that, some are, and those who are express it on social media every day. Some women simply don't agree with Beyoncé publicly displaying her sex appeal and think she needs to be more modest, more like a Sade. I can understand that concern for her or any woman's safety and any thinking person should. America is historically misogynistic, chauvinistic, [white] patriarchal and much of its low-brow citizenry still openly objectify, oppress and brutalize females/women with impunity. I talked about some of these standards in my article

Is Bill Cosby Innocent or Guilty? This concern for her or any woman's safety doesn't mean that I think women should wear scent neutral potato sacks to not set off the savages. It does mean that I think we need to work towards a paradigm shift in terms of better educating our young girls and boys about self respect and respect for each other. It also means that if we want to teach that respect we need to consistently demonstrate it in our everyday lives and help each other do the same. Some of us, men and women, are savages and aren't going to do anything about our level of respect. When this is the case, it's important for us to manage our children's expose to this and help insure this kind of mentality isn't poisoning the wishing well of our next generation. As our children become young adults, adults and then possibly parents, they will make their own decisions about what they agree and disagree with. For those of us who care, it is our job is to make sure that the legacy we're creating, and will ultimately leave behind, helps lead our future generations in the right direction.

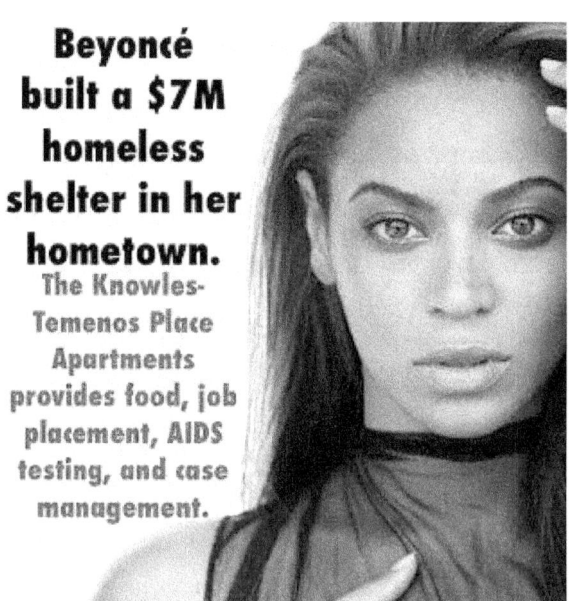

Beyoncé built a $7M homeless shelter in her hometown. The Knowles-Temenos Place Apartments provides food, job placement, AIDS testing, and case management.

In seeing events like Beyoncé's recent media storm, it all comes down to asking ourselves, "What are you going to do about it?" -regardless if we're Team Reaction or Team Responded. One of the things that I've always strongly advocated is to critique something with contributions. Everyone has an opinion yet everyone is not willing and able to offer anything above and beyond that opinion. That inactivity changes nothing, especially when that critique is negative, and that's a double whammy. Even if it's a positive critique, we can still do something above and beyond that opinion. For example, I like the Hip Hop artist Earl Sweatshirt who was a member of the group OFWGKTA. Not only are my critiques of his music generally positive, I literally support his brand; a took two youth to a concert, I exposed thousands of listeners to him by featuring his music on a Musicology Episode of my show Atlantis Build Talk Radio, and I purchased some of his music and merchandise. I may not like everything Earl Sweatshirt does but if I do, I support it, with more than an opinion. If I don't, and I publicly share that critique, I offer some contribution as an alternative. I likewise don't like everything Beyoncé does artistically yet there are some things I do. In 2013 I screened Bey's 'Life Is But A Dream' documentary for an International Woman's Day event I co-hosted and again in 2014 for 9-12 year old youth in my STYA Program. If you haven't seen the documentary I encourage you to check it out, it's very insightful and especially empowering for girls and women of color to see.

Seeing all of these critiques I contacted one of my sisters in Canada, Queen Cee, who among many other things she does as an artist/activist such as the Be-You-tiful Girls Club initiative, owns and operates a company called Queen Dollylama that creatively re-images dolls to give them a naturally unique, ethnic and artistic look. As there is a lacking of dolls that are Afrocentric, she also specializes in re-imaging dolls of color. My idea was to build upon the positive momentum of Beyoncé using part of her platform to project black consciousness and culture into the mainstream media and collaborate with Queen Cee to customize a collector's edition doll that reflects these ideals of black resistance, #blacklivesmatter, Black Panther homage and of course #Formation.

Queen Dollylama Beyoncé Formation doll

Once the customization was complete we held a global drawing for people to win it! People had until 11:59pm EST on March 8th {International Women's Day} to register and the drawing was held the following day. To register people simply had to:

1.) LIKE the 'Queen Dollylama' Facebook Page.
2.) LIKE the Picture on my Facebook Page.
3.) SHARE the Picture on their Facebook Page.

Although my main intention for this initiative was to build upon the positive momentum of Beyoncé using part of her platform to project black consciousness and culture into the mainstream media, the goal was twofold. First I wanted to show people creative ways to support each other through collaborations, especially using social networking. This project demonstrated what it means to "critique something with contributions" It's something I've done for years now and one of the main ideas I strive to communicate to people. It took very little effort and organizing to create this initiative that has effectively exposed thousands of more people to Queen Dollylama and A.S.I.A. To me, this demonstrates the power of collective work & responsibility and what social media should be positively used for, in contrast to empty debates, gossiping, fight videos, soft porn or other things. Secondly, because Queen Dollylama specializes in creatively re-imaging dolls to give them a naturally unique, ethnic and artistic look, especially Afrocentric, I want to encourage others to come up with ideas to develop their own Queen Dollylama customization for their children, nieces, cousins, friends and etc. Lastly, I planned this initiative for March to do my part in celebrating Women's History Month {March} and International Women's Day {March 8th}. Analytics wise, by using the hashtags #WomensHistoryMonth and #InternationalWomensDay in conjunction with #QueenDollylama #AtlantisBuild, #Beyoncé, #Formation, #BlackLivesMatter and etc. this gave our initiative even greater visibility to reach a larger audience. Events like Beyoncé and others breaking the internet in a positive way will continue to be landmark moments within the chronology of our people that shapes the human geography of this world, whether we like it or not. The bottom line is we must be mindful of our position of power to consistently control this narrative. Not with an opinion, with contributions that are purposeful and a positive part of our legacy. There were many participants in the Queen Dollylama Doll Giveaway from around the world and the lucky winner was a woman named Kali-Ma Imecca from Rochester, NY.

What about the black on black crime?

I despise it. I will that it never even comes close to the historical and present day white on white and white on black crime and violence we've historically seen and continue to see in this country.

Black people make up only about 12% of the U.S. population. White people make up about 63% of the U.S. population. Based upon sheer numbers alone it's practically impossible to rival the extent of white on white and white on black crime and violence that's perpetrated by 63% of the population among themselves, against black people and other minority groups in this country. I think it's a fair assessment to say that the crime and violence we see in any minority community in this country is a microcosmic example of a macrocosmic culture of violence expressed among the majority of our U.S. population.

Why do they fear the Devil?

Many of us are afraid. What is required of us, to end this now, many of us are afraid. Fear has many of us feeling paralyzed and powerless to bring about a change. Let's cease casting nets of false hope, fishing for minnows of mindfulness and morality, in a sea of indifference and indignation. Let's not continue to allow the death of a family member be the rare time we see each other, talk to each other and come together as one. There is only one real practical solution now and for the future: unify, protect one another and teach loving fearless children. The time is now.

Monday July 4th, 2016

Let me give you some context: Today, July 4th, 2016 America celebrates its 240th birthday. Of those 240 years, black people were not allowed to legally participate in American Society for 188 of those years. Although many of our ancesters were brought here in 1555 and enslaved for 221 years prior to Independence Day, from 1776 to 1865 this government continued slavery for another 89 years. From 1865 to 1964 this government then segregated black people for another 99 years. These 188 years are almost 80% (78.4%) of the time America has existed. That is approximately 6 generations of black people who were enslaved and segregated.

It doesn't take a person with x-ray vision to see that in the 52 years, alittle over 1 generation, black people have been allowed to legally participate in American Society, this hasn't entirely transformed the attitudes, institutions and government policies that many Americans have historically had towards black people whom they consider(ed) subhuman, inferior, second class and often criminal. Although this country has made some strides from 1964 -2016 to change things, we still have a long way to go -especially considering what we're seeing during this Election Year alone. I appreciate those of you who are striving to help bring about this change and rearing our children to be Ambassadors of that future. July 4th has many meanings to different people and this is just one perspective. A perspective from one who descended from some of the most resilient people who gained some semblance of American independence 188 years later, on July 2nd, 1964.

Musth too Much

In the animal world, males typically demonstrate various forms of physiological pageantry to 'show-off' their so-called dominance to each other and onlooking females. Whether it's flashing bright colors like golden-headed lion tamarins, butting heads like big horn sheep or singing sophisticated songs like a lyre bird, male animals, obviously in their primal state, thrive on competition. The same can be said for male humans -who have not evolved beyond our primal reptilian brain function. Cognitively speaking, there is no difference between a raging bull elephant during musth or a raging male talking bull...

Five Percenter
Table Talks
Featuring: Author Paul L. Guthrie

I recently had an opportunity to build with Author Paul Lawrence Guthrie about his book Making of the Whiteman, his documentary series via the World Dhamma Foundation and various other sciences of life. We've agreed to make a portion of our dialogue available to the public. There are Five Percenter newborns, others within our Nation and members of other conscious groups who are not familiar with his contributions in regards to KOS [Knowledge of Self]. I wanted to highlight some of those contributions. Also, over the years the Five Percenters have often been labeled Muslims and Mr. Guthrie's work, particularly clarifying some of the source material of the Nation of Islam's teachings and 120 lessons, has been very helpful in addressing this label. Do the knowledge!

Saladin Allah: The first time I heard of you was back in the 90's and it was through a book you published entitled "Making of the Whiteman: History, Tradition and the Teachings of Elijah Muhammad." That book was a staple for those of us coming into knowledge of self before the proliferation of the internet and social media. Even today, and almost twenty-five years later, that book is still considered a literary classic. What prompted you to write that book and how do you see it almost twenty-five years later?

Paul Guthrie: At that time, a lot of the literature on the topic was religious in nature and I wanted to write something non-religious. I wanted the book to be short enough to read in one day; with over-sized type, to reduce eye strain; and to use plain words, so as to be understandable to everyday people. I'm happy that the book has held up well, over time.

Saladin Allah: True indeed. In addition to the book itself one of the best parts to me were the numerous sources you cited in the back. I read the book in one day yet invested many days researching the sources. Some of the books I found in my local library hadn't been taken out in almost twenty years. With the development and expansion of the internet, we now have a Millennial Generation born as social media natives. For many, web surfing and social networking has begun to replace the traditional fact finding missions of exploring local libraries, bookstores, visiting people and etc. to gain knowledge. What does this technological paradigm shift mean for our present and future generations? How does this shift positively and/or negatively effect one's journey who is seeking knowledge?

Paul Guthrie: Those references were used with the hope that people might go on to further reading. The way you used the book was exactly what I had in mind.

Since the rise of the internet, literacy has been in decline. And even literacy itself, is changing. Reading words printed on paper (in books) is a different process than reading online. When I first began to read online I had to almost re-learn the kind of thought processes used while reading from books. It took me several months to re-learn how to mentally process online information. Computers throw the information at you at a different speed and with a different flavor. It's not the same; it comes at you from a different angle. I promote that people use paper printed books (while they're still available), and maybe supplement their reading with online sources.

I'm not very familiar with most of the social media. However, I think it's safe to say that following the shift towards social media, people are becoming less social. Maybe computers should be used in moderation.

Saladin Allah: Since the release of your book I see that you've been able to successfully use this 'medium' to present something called The World Dhamma Foundation. What is the World Dhamma Foundation and how did it come about?

Paul Guthrie: Dhamma means reality. Dhamma is the word used in Buddhist circles to describe things as they are, as well as to describe the science or method leading to the attainment of insight into those things. Dhamma is a scientific discipline rooted in personal experience. World Dhamma Foundation promotes the study and practice of Dhamma (Buddhism).

Saladin Allah: Several years ago in 2008 through the World Dhamma Foundation you began to share a series of videos related to your research on W.D. Fard, also known as Master Fard Muhammad; co-founder of the Nation of Islam. In those videos you elaborate in detail on his origins in India, not Arabia and his teachings correlation to Buddhism, not Islam. How did you begin to make these correlations and what in particular within the Supreme Wisdom book and specific degrees within 120 lessons made you come to this conclusion?

Paul Guthrie: My Supreme Wisdom lessons come literally from a garbage can, from the alley behind Muhammad's Temple #8. The Temple threw them away in the 1970's. I lived a few blocks away, near 25th and Imperial and I still have those lessons today. The Temple was located across the street from what had once been the local chapter of the Black Panther Party.

The 120 or Supreme Wisdom lessons is a coherent body of teachings. A pattern or paradigm. In my view, Buddhist principles and practices run throughout the lessons from start to finish. When I look at the terminology used throughout them; as well as the principles and practices, they are consistent throughout with Buddhism. I think it's significant that W. D. Fard mentions no Islamic principles or practices. If we call the lessons "Islam" we should know it's very different from what the rest of the world calls Islam. And it's okay to do so, however for me it seems more coherent to refer to those principles and practices as perfectly consistent with Dhamma.

Saladin Allah: It's interesting you mention that because a similar paradigm shift took place with the branch of the Nation of Islam under the leadership of Minister Louis Farrakhan fairly recently. Over the last decade his Department of Supreme Wisdom stopped issuing official copies of the Supreme Wisdom book and consequently the lessons. His controversial Scientology campaign directing his believers to get audited at its church and study Dianetics also came a short time after this.

In your videos about W.D. Fard you talked about how the lessons only mention about a few Islamic words in comparison to ten thousand other words, and not in a traditional Muslim context. Another point you elaborated on, in addition to Fard's handwriting being Urdu, not Arabic, is that in his 'Instructions to the Laborers' he specifically defined the teachings as "mixed." In my own research I also found correlations between some of the lessons and what Madame HP Blavatsky taught within the Theosophy Society such as her being educated by hidden masters in the East during the time of Fard's childhood, the 25,000 calendar and etc. Did you also come across these correlations? What other correlations did you find throughout these "mixed" teachings other than Buddhism?

Paul Guthrie: Yes, in the lessons you can see evidence of the trends of that time. And as you've noted, Blavatsky's Theosophical Movement is one such trend. Blavatsky's Isis Unveiled was published in 1877, and the same is officially recognized as W. D. Fard's birth year. Blavatsky is said to have borrowed the title Isis Unveiled, from the title of Anacalypsis, by Godfrey Higgins. The full title is: "Anacalypsis: An Attempt to Draw Aside the Veil of the Saitic Isis or an Inquiry into the Origin of Languages, Nations and Religions." It's reported that W. D. Fard frequently used the text Anacalypsis during his talks. Both Anacalypsis and Isis Unveiled focus on Buddhist India.

Regarding groups ceasing to issue the Supreme Wisdom lessons: maybe they believe they've exhausted the value contained in those lessons. Sometimes religious organizations ban or otherwise de-emphasize their source material for political reasons. Ancient Rome's conversion to Christianity is one such example. In the case of Christianity, many of the early texts were banned following the Roman conversion. Rome did that for political reasons. The Gnostic school (Knowledge) was replaced by the newly Romanized, Pistos school (Faith). In politics and in religion, authority tends to flow uphill. Outside of politics and religion, authority normally rests with the individual. I think the lessons speak of that dynamic and guard against it - where the Instructions say, "I do not want importance among the Laborers nor Officials."

I mention the 25,000-year processional calendar cycle and the trillion-plus calendar year system in Part One of the documentary series. I plan to talk about a lot of other correlations in Parts Three and Four.

Saladin Allah: Much of what you say conflicts with what people are traditionally taught about Fard and the lessons. What has been the general consensus from those who have been exposed to your research? How has your research been received by the different branches of the Nation of Islam? And I ask because many people are unaware that there are multiple "Nations" of Islam with various leaders such as the late John Muhammad [Elijah's brother], Silias Muhammad, Solomon Royall, The Son of Man [Marvin Muhammad], Ahmad A. Muhammad, Minister Louis Farrakhan and others.

Paul Guthrie: Most of the people from whom I've heard have been open to the ideas. I think they're exceptional in that they probably don't represent the general consensus.

There are a number of Nation of Islam organizations. I don't know that any of those organizations have received the Get On Board The Wheel documentary series in a welcoming way.

Outside of the people who are already studying with us, the most positive reception has been from the Five Percent. I value their responses. Especially the older Gods -- many of them already know what I'm talking about. Additionally, I've heard from many rank-and-file Nation of Islam members; some of them have been very supportive. I value their support too.

Saladin Allah: Your research is what sparked a public dialogue and inspired various people to research, write about, lecture and even publicly debate the correlation between Indian or Indus Valley teachings and the original source material of the Supreme Wisdom book and 120 lessons. As Five Percenters, we are scientists of life, not religious or dogmatic. This is one of the reasons many of us appreciate you; you've added on and continue to add on knowledge to our cipher. Because we are not Muslims and don't base our worldview on a belief system, in our quest for knowledge we strive to be right and exact and stand to be corrected if we're not. If I'm building with another Five Percenter or anybody that's sharing information that either conflicts with or adds onto what I previously learned, I'm open to researching and integrating it into my life if it's right and exact. That attitude and posture is a vital part of the growth and development process.

Although change can be challenging for any of us, I think it's very difficult for most religious people because their foundation is belief, not knowledge. In regards to those who have been the most oppositional to your research, what have you found to be the most problematic for them to accept? What have you learned from this opposition and how have you addressed it?

Paul Guthrie: I agree with you on that, in real dialogue everyone wins. Also, I have tried to keep up with your builds for a number of years now. Your builds are informative and very solid. You teach by example Saladin and many people (including myself) benefit from that example.

As far as certain people opposing or not accepting particular ideas - I'm open to that. So far, the main opposition has been emotional opposition. I don't see much evidence-based opposition. I suspect that over time the emotional responders will piece together a more coherent opposition. Those kind of emotional reactions are "magnetic", it's just a way to throw us off course. In Dhamma practices, the magnetic is called clinging and aversion – if you watch, when someone reacts to an issue emotionally, you can see they're trying to push you or pull you in one direction or the other – to turn you away from the issue. I'm open to critique and to dialogue and learning. I certainly don't advocate that people agree with a thing until after they've thoroughly looked into it for themselves.

Saladin Allah: I appreciate that my brother and I'm honored that I've been able to add-on. Your mention of "magnetic" reminds me of the 22nd lesson in the 1-40. As you know, it talks about Yacub discovering magnetic while playing with two pieces of steel as a child. Within that discovery Yacub learned that the piece with the magnetic attracted the piece without. As it correlates to people, it was the piece/people without magnetic who were pushed or pulled and easily led in one direction or the other that the devil was eventually made manifest through. It was also this manifestation that eventually threw the entire human family off course. I've definitely witnessed and experienced various forms of emotional opposition and knee-jerk reactions to knowledge, especially in the form of social media trolling nowadays. If it occurs I've always strived to not go there because it's nothing more than a proverbial island of Pelon where people are made other than themselves.

Right now you've made Get On Board The Wheel Part One and Get On Board The Wheel Part Two documentary series available to the public and are currently working on Part Three. What other projects can we look forward to from The

World Dhamma Foundation and are you currently working on any future books?

Paul Guthrie: That's true, I've followed your builds for a number of years. I'm not surprised to hear that. It reminds me of the classic, WWII bomber pilot saying, "If you're receiving fire, it only means you're over the target." Keep dropping that knowledge brother.

I do plan to put a few things in book form. Any future books will be free of charge. It's easy today to make ebooks without any overhead charges. I'm currently able to convert literature into epub, mobi and pdf formats. Under the current circumstances, it's far easier for me to produce and easier to distribute in digital formats. If people prefer, they can print them onto paper. That's how I plan to handle any future literature (free of charge).

The Get On Board The Wheel series is preparatory to the Dhamma Talks series. I want to share a view of Dhamma specifically tailored on our culture, using our language and our dialect. Alongside the Dhamma Talks series will be other series.

Saladin Allah: That's excellent to hear and I'm sure many of us are looking forward to that. Over the last decade I've seen people use some of your research to self publish books, do paid lectures and public debates. I've even heard that your book "Making of the Whiteman: History, Tradition and the Teachings of Elijah Muhammad" has been reprinted and sold without your authorization.

As there is a fine line between sharing knowledge and monetizing what we do as researchers, authors, consultants and etc., why have you chosen to share The Get On Board The Wheel series, the Dhamma Talks series and future literature for free as opposed to selling it at a reasonable cost?

Paul Guthrie: The information is free. Books, DVD's, information or services from me are free of charge.

Saladin Allah: If it's true that your book has been reprinted and sold without your authorization, how have you addressed this in regards to your intellectual property rights?

Paul Guthrie: The last "authorized" version was in 1996 (around that time). Nearly all the copies since then have been bootleg versions (with the exception of maybe 1 or 2). A few years ago a friend asked me if he could publish a few thousand copies (he owns KHA Books). That's probably the only "authorized" printing in nearly the last 20 years. I'm not charging him for those. I still own the intellectual property rights to the book and I do know who the bootleggers have been. I have generally responded to the bootleggers on a case-by-case basis.

Saladin Allah: I definitely understand and I will that you continue to address that. At one point an article I wrote was being used without my authorization as the forward to a book of lessons being sold on Amazon. It took some research but I was finally able to track down the author through his publishing company and get Amazon to stop selling copies and him to re-edit the book. It was a nightmare, seeing that we as Five Percenters don't sell our lessons.

Well Brother, our interview has drawn to close and I want to thank you again for this opportunity to build. Where can my readers stay connected to your continual work with The World Dhamma Foundation and is there anything else that you would like to share before you go?

Paul Guthrie: Thank you Saladin and thank you to your readers.

Paul can be reached at:
Paul@WorldDhammaFoundation.com

The Flint Water Crisis
#FlintLivesMatter

On January 16th, 2016 President Obama declared a federal state of emergency in Flint Michigan because of its polluted water. Residents there cannot bathe in or drink the water, all children under the age of six have been exposed to lead poisoning and the national guard has been called in to help facilitate the process of getting clean/donated water to the people.

According to USA Today Network Journalist Jessica Durrando, *"Flint's drinking water became contaminated with lead in April 2014 while the city was under the control of a state-appointed emergency manager. As a cost-cutting move, the city began temporarily drawing its drinking water from the Flint River and treating it at the city water treatment plant while it waited for a new water pipeline to Lake Huron to be completed. Previously, the city used Lake Huron water treated by the Detroit Water and Sewerage Department. The state Department of Environmental Quality has conceded it failed to require needed chemicals to be added to the corrosive Flint River water. As a result, lead leached from pipes and fixtures into the drinking water."*

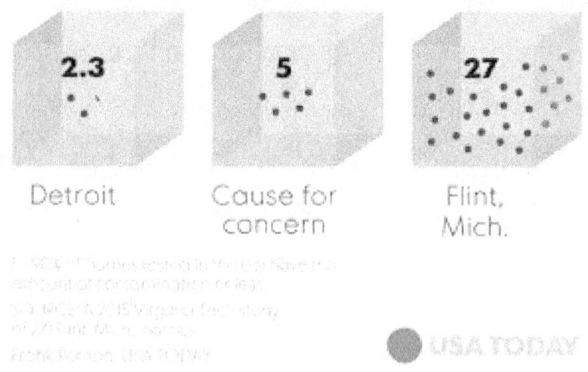

LEAD LEVEL COMPARISONS

Water contamination in Flint, Mich., compared with that of Detroit – Flint's original source for purified water.

90th percentile¹ levels of lead exposure (in parts per billion):

| 2.3 | 5 | 27 |
| Detroit | Cause for concern | Flint, Mich. |

USA TODAY

Michigan Gov. Rick Snyder who has been singled out as dropping the ball of this has stated for the record, *"I'm sorry and I will fix it,"* and *"Government failed you at the federal, state and local level."* Aside from apologies, what are the short and long term solutions to solving this problem that has effected so many lives, especially our children? Like with many stories we see circulating in the news, some people view a crisis like this as having nothing to do with them. I beg to differ and refer you to the words of Dr. Martin Luther King who said, *"Injustice anywhere is a threat to justice everywhere."*

In Niagara Falls, NY we had one of the worst environmental tragedies in American history happen in community called the Love Canal. From the early 1940's to the mid-1950's Hooker Chemical Company, with government sanction, began using a partially dug canal as a chemical waste dump which equated to almost 22,000 tons of toxic waste being buried there. After covering the site with dirt and selling the land to the Niagara Falls Board of Education for $1 with a disclaimer, construction of a school and homes eventually began on this site. By the 1970's this landfill was in proximity to approximately 800 single family homes, 240 low-income apartments and a public elementary school. It was also during the late 1970's that complaints of odors and substances seeping through the ground were taken seriously and it was discovered that toxic vapors and the contents from this chemical landfill began to were indeed seeping into the drinking water, soil and basements of the residents, for years. This exposure was linked to everything from asthma, seizures, cancer, miscarriages, birth defects and various other issues. As with present day Flint Michigan, President Jimmy Carter declared a federal state of emergency in 1978 and some of the families were evacuated. A second federal state of emergency was declared by President Carter in 1981 to relocate the other families after being pressured by activists.

Like Flint Michigan, all municipalities, including the one where you live, cut costs and/or corners when it comes to its citizens. Publically it's called "balancing the budget", privately it's oftentimes a very different conversation. In Flint Michigan, that cost/corner cutting, or should I say neglect, was in the area of waste water treatment/management. In your city it may be the school district. Somewhere else it may be infrastructure. Other places it's a combination of cut costs/corners, especially when a large segment of its population is poor, disenfranchised, unemployed or uneducated. In many cases these communities are primarily people of color.

While some of your local and regional public officials are striving to do their best to serve you, many are not for various reasons. Sometimes they're self serving and aren't concerned about the citizens. Sometimes they lack a consensus among their peers to get something done. Sometimes they lack civic engagement or valuable input from their citizens. Most times there are layers of cost/corner cutting among city employees, department heads, city administrators, contractors and etc. that public officials have to strive to deal with, if they're not a part of the problem. As the crisis in Flint unfolds, the blame game has also commenced. Although Michigan Gov. Rick Snyder must be held responsible for this water crisis, he did not act alone and public officials on the regional and local level must be held accountable too.

This should be more than a wake-up call for us to become more civically engaged where we live. As citizens, we are not immune to neglect. If you or anyone you know wants to help the families in Flint with a monetary donation, you can do so at this website: The Community Foundation of Greater Flint [CFGF]. The city is striving to streamline financial efforts through the Community Foundation of Greater Flint; a 501(c)(3) nonprofit organization and your gift is tax deductible to the extent allowed by law.

Is Bill Cosby Innocent or Guilty?

Since the rape allegations against Bill Cosby have come out, people have also come out on both sides offering their perspectives on his innocence or guilt. Some have framed it as a white supremacist witch hunt to destroy the black father image. Others have viewed it as a man getting off easy, pun intended, because of his celebrity status. What many are not saying, or taking a look at, is the cultural context or backdrop these alleged incidents happened on or the mainstream medium they're being discussed in. What do I mean by that?

When you look at Bill Cosby's comedy career, on different occasions he's done comedy bits about slipping women a mickey; drugging women. He did it in live stand-ups, on his comedy album it's true! it's true! and on Larry King Live in 1991. This doesn't mean that he actually did these things but it does mean that this was something that his audience related to; it was an obvious part of popular culture, especially in Hollywood, going back to the 1960's where these incidents date back to. In terms of popular American culture, some of its background music historically reflects this notion about its drug culture. There was a very popular song covered by various rock, country and etc. artists called Quaaludes Again you can listen to on Youtube.

Post WWII in the 1950's America saw an expanse of drug use that was articulated in a popular Hollywood film called The Man With The Golden Arm starring Frank Sinatra, who was speculated to be a cocaine business partner of Colombian drug lord Pablo Escobar. Even when you look at the backdrop of 1960's drug culture, including Jazz music, it's rare to find jazz artists who didn't have contact with drugs. Many died from this. In the 1970's you see it's continuation with popular heroin addict songs like Neil Young's The Needle And The Damage, Gil Scott Heron's Home Is Where The Hatred Is and novels like Faggots where the characters are constantly doing Quaaludes as a party drug used in New York gay community before the popularization of AIDS. Even in the 1980's you see it the popular film Scarface when Tony referred to his wife's drug addiction, the coming of crack and President Reagan's so-called War On Drugs campaign. This type of popular American culture continued on into the 90's and 2000's and cannot be trivialized or overlooked when considering the context of the Cosby allegations. Being a Hollywood staple for many years, Cosby and many others most certainly had contact with the drug culture. Hollywood wasn't in a vacuum nor a place in an alternate universe disconnected from popular American drug culture. Because of this, it's rare to find any comedians, actors, musicians and people working in the entertainment business who didn't have contact with drugs. With the new designer drugs of today, coupled with various drugs of yesterday, I think it's still rare to find comedians, actors, musicians and people working in the entertainment business, especially in Hollywood, who don't have contact with drugs. This has been a part and continues to be a part of popular American culture. A popular American culture that some of the present day corporate sponsored rap artists have now become one of its biggest advocates of.

Herein lies a fundamental problem; Popular drug culture is superimposed over a racist and sexist [misogyny and chauvinism] American backdrop. This is a problem that many of us overlook, ignore and ultimately fail to address. What this translates into are people of color and women being victimized in/by a system we may or may not choose to participate in. In the case of Bill Cosby we see this being played out on two fronts. First we see him being used as the face of popular American drug culture, which he is not. Yes it's possible that he sexually assaulted women in his past and got away with it because of his celebrity status and the fact that he is a male. It's possible that some of these women were active participants or outright lying. It's also a fact that various others were doing this, especially white male celebrities, yet they have not been demonized in the same way Cosby is. Take Roman Polanski for example, the famous director, producer, writer and actor who drugged and raped a thirteen-year-old at Jack Nicholson's house. He plead guilty to the charge of "Unlawful Sexual Intercourse with a minor" and in 1988 he agreed to pay her $500,000 plus interest based upon a civil suit. This and countless examples show you there's a contradiction here.

Secondly we see the marginalization of women living in a misogynistic society that mirrors ancient Rome and women in the Victorian era. Because of this, females/women are devalued, objectified and their issues trivialized. Take for example the recent public outrage surrounding the Rick Ross album Black Market that was pulled from Walmart's website because the song Free Enterprise had Anti-George Zimmerman/Donald Trump lyrics. In it Ross raps, *"Assassinate Trump like I'm Zimmerman/Now accept these words as they came from Eminem."* This is the same Rick Ross who was slapped on the wrist for his rape rap verse, *"Put molly all in her champagne, she ain't even know it/I took her home and I enjoyed that/She ain't even know it"* on the Rocko song U.O.E.N.O. While he was kicked off of the public campaign to represent the Reebok brand at the time, he is still the face of its Rebook CrossFit training program he remixed as #RossFit. What this and various scenarios sadly demonstrate is that females/women, especially ones of color, being violated, unacknowledged and not protected comes along with the territory in a historically sexist [misogynistic and chauvinistic] society. Now I've heard the argument that some or many of the women accusing Bill Cosby of sexual assault are hoes who were trying to f*ck their way to the top. Well even if this was the case, based upon your definition of a hoe or even a woman who proudly calls herself a hoe, even a so-called hoe has the right to be conscious and coherent while she's f*cking her way to the top. In other words, at no point is it alright to take advantage of any female/woman or male/man, without or even with, their consent, period. Unfortunately, this attitude towards human life has gone on since America's unsavory inception, up until today. In addition to looking at what's happening with these allegations, another problem is people don't want to look at the sick system that helps produce, protect and perpetuate these dysfunctional behaviors.

I don't anticipate or expect this narrative to be discussed along with the Cosby sexual assault allegations. Nor do I expect some cataclysmic shift in the American culture that continues to produce, protect and perpetuate dysfunction. This would require a system to indict itself. Has Bill Cosby received celebrity privileges surrounding these allegations? Absolutely, and this is a problem. Is he being treated differently than his white counterparts who've had sexual allegations or plead guilty to sex offenses? Absolutely, and this is a problem. Are victims or alleged victims of sexual abuse, especially females/women, blamed for what happened to them and/or slut shammed? Absolutely, and this is a problem. Has there been a popular American drug culture going on since the 1960's up until today that has shaped every aspect of this society, including the commentary surrounding these allegations? Absolutely, and this is a problem too. In analyzing what's going on I would encourage people to not get sucked into an emotional game on a lopsided field governed with unfair rules, covered by unfair commentators and funded by unfair sponsors. In the end, nobody wins but them, unless we're wise enough to not play their game. Whether Bill Cosby gets convicted of something or not, the popular American culture is still here and we'll see more people like him in the news. Whether some of the women who've accused him of sexual assault are proven to be true, the popular American culture is still here and we'll see more people like them in the news. As we critique these allegations and determine what needs to be done based upon the findings of facts, we must also examine the areas in this cultural system that need to be revamped that makes drug and rape culture acceptable. This is especially important for our youth -who are being shaped and molded into the image and likeness of this kind of culture.

The Original Woman and Planet Earth

The Earth's magnetic relationship with the Moon's 28-day lunar cycle effects our planet's tides the same way a woman's 28-day menstrual cycle effects her emotional tides that are linked to her sympathetic nervous system that partly regulates her hormones and body's ability to cope with stress. As hunter gatherers that eventually transitioned into agriculture and industrialism, we directly consulted with women who were biologically in tune with our landscape, planting and harvest seasons. As forecasters, their wisdom and guidance was critical to our survival and that consultation also corresponds to the creation of calendars based upon a 28 lunar and her 28-day menstrual cycle. Among many societies, a woman is seen as an Oracle [diviner] within its cultural matrix because of her intuition, our southern relatives call "mother wit" and what

Western Philosophy has come to define as priori knowledge. In Greece for example, she was the priestess Pythia; central figure of the Gaia [Earth] society and Oracle of Delphi men would consult for guidance on the seventh day of each month.

Dec 12, 2015 10:45am

I'm not sure if some of you are aware but there's a Renaissance of consciousness happening around college campuses today where many of our Millennial Generation are looking back at media contributions like A Different World and drawing inspiration from its social justice insights, fashion ideas and cultural orientation.

THO[ugh]TS

GIRL [10 yr old]: He's a THOT. Guys can be a THOT too.
ME: Yeah, guys are the first "THOT."
GIRL: Huh?
ME: There would be no such thing as a THOT if guys didn't start it.

The RZA
Bloomberg Interview

In a recent interview on the with-all-due-respect segment of Bloomberg Politics, Wu-Tang Clan frontman Prince Rakeem Allah, AKA The RZA, spoke on #blacklivesmatter, police brutality, the black male image, Donald Trump and the 2016 Presidential Election that some have praised and criticized him about. If you have not seen parts of this interview you can view it on Youtube by searching RZA Bloomberg Politics Interview.

With the growth and development of the Social Media Age, everyone now has a public figure platform. A platform where whatever we say or do can be held for or against us in a court of law and in the court of public opinion. I've seen people get arrested or fired from their jobs because of a Facebook status. I've seen companies loose money because of a video. I've watched celebrities get shunned because of a snapshotted tweet they tried to delete. Aside from net worth, there's a very thin line that separates celebrities from everyday people. At any given moment, you as an everyday person can end up going viral because of something and be catapulted into the national or even international spotlight. When this has happened, most are completely unprepared and this serves one lopsided purpose: the media's ratings, web traffic and analytics data that drives economic trends. One of the main concerns I've had and have worked to address is the lacking or non-existence of effective PR representation for black/brown people, and any group that's considered a minority, when we're engaging the mainstream media -especially celebrities. Whether it's LeBron James being asked about the Tamir Rice case and his response that he hasn't been on top of it, Young Thug's response to being asked about police brutality and even Dej Loaf saying she had no clue who Boss was when I interviewed her in Toronto, this unpreparedness coupled with a lack of PR representation is not working in our best interest. The idea of news reporters looking around for the black person in the shower cap to interview is over. Now the media has learned effective tactics to shower cap people they choose to interview.

In all of the responses I've seen about RZA's Interview, whether pro or con, it amazed me how so many people had an opinion without ever questioning the actual context and forum this interview was conducted in. First and foremost, that interview was conducted by Bloomberg L.P.; a global business, financial information and news company. Bloomberg has over a quarter of a million professional service subscribers and approximately one million business week subscribers in over 150 countries. Demographically speaking, their target audience are not Millennials, nor do they look like RZA, his 6ft 4in son, or any of us voicing our opinion. Over 85% are middle age white men with money. This is to say that many of us weren't invited to that Bloomberg conversation. RZA was speaking to a middle aged white journalist with money to other middle aged white men with money, and a lot of what he had to say was agreeable with them.

Now, here's the fundamental problem with many of us, such as RZA, who speak to audiences like this that don't reflect the minority group we're a part of, regardless how American we claim to be: we don't consider the audience and who we're talking to. As a Guest Columnist for my local paper I wrote an article in December of 2014 entitled "Of course 'All Lives Matter" in response to the blacklash the Black Lives Matter movement began to receive. Ironically, it's the same "of course all lives matter" quote RZA used in his interview yet we both took very different approaches in articulating it. Because the primary subscribers to the local paper where I live are also middle age whites, I know the audience I'm communicating to and commit myself to sharing a unique perspective that's usually not represented and/or respected in their mainstream media. In reading my article above and knowing their primary audience, ask yourself what purpose does that article serve them. In listening to RZA's interview and knowing Bloomberg's primary audience, ask yourself what purpose did that interview possibly serve them. Is that demographic more conscious of the legitimate challenges black/brown people and other minority groups deal with in regards to police brutality? Does that demographic know anything more about the valid criticisms black/brown people and other minority groups have about Donald Trump's or Hillary Clinton's policies? Do you think Bloomberg's audience received commentary that would help them become more aware and sensitive to the perspectives of black/brown people and other minority groups?

Some of us that simply agreed with RZA's commentary are equivalent to janitors cleaning up an office, overhearing parts of a conversation about us in an executive boardroom by a black man with white executives around him and butting into the conversation to voice our opinion. Let me reiterate that this interview was by Bloomberg L.P for its share holders and subscribers, not for us -even though we were being discussed. After this interview was edited and shared with their primary share holders and subscribers, then it was shared with us; the outsiders. Many of our unsolicited opinions are only used to reinforce and quantify that conversation by a black man with white executives around him in that boardroom. Some of us who voiced our opinion have not even researched Bloomberg L.P. or their founders. As Five Percenters who pride ourselves on "doing the knowledge" first, I find this especially alarming and unscientific. While all of us Five Percenters are entitled to an opinion, this is precisely why many of us are completely unqualified to speak for us as a collective. At least know the medium you're speaking through first, who their primary audience is and then what purpose your commentary will serve. Bloomberg L.P. was founded in 1981 by four men who were all colleagues at Salomon Brothers, one of the biggest trading and investment houses on Wall Street until they transitioned into Morgan Stanley -one of the companies that was given $10 billion during the government bail out that helped spark the Occupy [Wall Street] Movement and concept of the 1% controlling the world's wealth. Both Salomon Brothers and Morgan Stanley have been in the midst of financial scandals since their inception.

Michael Bloomberg: Former Mayor of New York who was first elected as a Democratic in 2001 yet changed party affiliations for the next 15 years to Republican and its minor party Independent. With a net worth of $39.3 billion, Bloomberg defines himself as a Fiscal Conservative and he was publically endorsed by Rupert Murdoch if he decided to run for President. Murdoch is the Republican face behind Fox News and its affiliates.

Thomas Secunda: A Jewish mathematician with a background in computer programming and fixed income trading. With a net worth of $1.91 billion, Secunda is also a philanthropist who funds various Environment, Arts & Culture, Education, Health organizations such as the American Israel Education Foundation, American Jewish

Joint Distribution and the UJA Federation: all affiliates with the Pro-Israeli anti-Palestinian AIPAC [American Israel Public Affairs Committee].

Duncan MacMillan: A mathematician and investment banker, MacMillan and his wife Nancy are endowed faculty chairs at Rutgers University which means they provide permanent funding to the University for "genomic" research; a branch of biotechnology that applies the techniques of genetics and molecular biology to the genetic mapping and DNA sequencing of sets of genes. While his net worth is unknown, it's speculated that he's worth at least $300 million.

Charles Zeger: Also Jewish, Zeger has a masters degree in computer science and has a net worth of $1.46 billion and made his money by developing the software for Bloomberg. Founder of the Zeger Family Foundation, Zeger and his wife Merryl are the only trustees who keep their grant funding broad and donate to many things. While their foundation accepts unsolicited ideas, they do not accept unsolicited grant proposals.

Geopolitically and socioeconomically, that says a lot. The criticism RZA has received is primarily coming from black/brown people and other minority group's whose

115

issues were under represented or not represented in his commentary, including Wu-Tang fans. However, Conservatives, Animal Rights Activists, Vegans, Patriots [Americans], Taoists and Law Enforcement were. That is a legitimate criticism I find problematic anytime a member of a minority group doesn't utilize their public platform to include the legitimate concerns of that group, especially in a mainstream medium where that perspective is usually not represented and/or respected. Another thing that was problematic is how non-indictments and police brutality against children like Tamir Rice, women like Sandra Bland and others that don't fit the black man profile wasn't addressed. They weren't men and their deaths had nothing to do with attire, dressing more refined and cleaning themselves up. Their deaths also had nothing to do with invoked fear. Saying to black males they need to take more responsibility for cleaning up their image, how law enforcement stereotypes them and it can contribute to police brutality is one thing. Saying to middle age white men with money that black males need to take more responsibility for cleaning up their image, how law enforcement stereotypes them and it can contribute to police brutality is something different. Either RZA knows what I'm speaking about and chose to speak in the best interest of the Bloomberg L.P share holders and subscribers or he doesn't know what I'm speaking about which means he's not as politically sophisticated as he needs to be before conducting interviews like this. As a man of knowledge, I'm sure that he's learning something from the public and private response to his interview. I also will that we are learning something too.

The Problem with Words

The words "female" and "male" are both technical, clinical and non-descriptive terms. That is how I specifically use them; as distinct synonyms to describe a person's self perception and state of growth and development. When people primarily identify/express themselves as an object [material/form], especially sexually, they're functioning as females and males. They're operating more from the baser "reptilian" [primitive/instinctive] brain function as opposed to higher cerebral cortex development. So female and male does not refer to 'sentient beings'; woman and man. It generally tells you nothing about their sense of humanity because female and male refers to gender and that can be any plant or animal. Also consider the fact that 'girl' is the only word that does not contain or imply the proximity to a man. LADy, woMAN, feMALE, woMEN, sHE and HEr do. The deeper we dig we'll discover that there are many words within the English dialect that people use everyday that become self imposed conceptual prison houses.

@AtlantisBuild

Unmasking White Domestic Terrorism

Colorado Springs, Colorado -On Friday November 27th, 2015 Christian Extremist and Domestic Terrorist Robert Lewis Dear, described by neighbors as a chronic complainer and "angry" "aloof" man "you had to watch out for", was given a choice to surrender to law enforcement after shooting up a Planned Parenthood clinic and murdering three people. Nine others were also hospitalized from his savage attack; five officers and four civilians. Although the mainstream media claims Dear's motive was unclear, a law enforcement official did confirm that Dear mentioned "no more baby parts" and expressed anti-abortion and anarchist [anti-government] views in interviews with authorities. Among some of his past criminal charges, Dear was charged with two counts of animal cruelty, being a peeping Tom and domestic assault against his wife. One of Dear's neighbors, Zigmond Post, also confirmed that Dear once brought him anti-Obama pamphlets.

While black/brown people are being murdered in cold blood by law enforcement for everything from simply wearing a hoodie, having our hands up, walking down the street, not being able to breathe, listening to music, playing at a playground and not using a turn signal, then demonized in the mainstream media as guilty until proven innocent, monsters like Robert Lewis Dear are normally innocent until proven guilty. In fact, after Dylann Roof murdered nine people in a church, law enforcement bought him Burger King after safely taking him into custody. This is a choice and consideration that Laquan McDonald and countless other black/brown people were never given, even when there was no evidence of a crime being committed. What this translates into is this: a double standard with two sets of judgment rules. One set of rules for black/brown people and another set of rules for black/brown people.

What do President Woodrow Wilson's Official White House screening of Birth of a Nation on March 21st, 1915 which celebrates the domestic terrorism of the KKK [Klu Klux

Klan], the domestic terrorism that burned down Black Wall Street and murdered approximately 1,000 black people in 16 hours during the Tulsa Race Riot, the generations of lynchings of black/brown people, Without Sanctuary, at the hands of domestic terrorist mobs, the countless school shootings carried out by domestic terrorists and the coddling claim that domestic terrorist Dylann Roof is "suspected of perpetrating" the murder of nine Charleston, SC church members, including State Senator Clementa C. Pinckley, all have in common? The mainstream media's refusal to unmask and categorize its Micheal Myers demographic as White Domestic Terrorists. And in case you didn't notice, this continues to be the consistent American non-narrative since its Native American genocidal inception.

In a Huffington Post article When The Media Treats White Suspects And Killers Better Than Black Victims writer Nick Wing elaborates, "*News reports often headline claims from police or other officials that appear unsympathetic or dismissive of black victims. Other times, the headlines seem to suggest that black victims are to blame for their own deaths, engaging in what critics sometimes allege is a form of character assassination. When contrasted with media portrayal of white suspects and accused murderers, the differences are more striking. News outlets often choose to run headlines that exhibit an air of disbelief at an alleged* white killer's supposed actions. Sometimes, they appear to go out of their way to boost the suspect's character, carrying quotes from relatives or acquaintances that often paint even alleged murderers in a positive light."

To add fuel to the fire, many Pro-Dear Extremists came out praising him for his heinous act:

I wonder how many unborn babies were save by this gunman interrupting normal Planned Parenthood activities? Just looking on the bright-side

11/27/15, 5:35 PM

planned parenthood kills a million babies and no one bats an eye. but 1 brave hero tries to put a stop to that, everyone loses their minds

3:31 PM - 27 Nov 2015

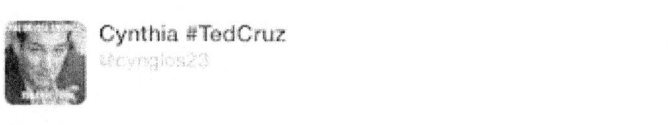

Cynthia #TedCruz
@cynglos23

@theblaze #PlannedParenthood no mention of how many babies lives were saved??? Such a shame but good things often come from tragedy.

11/27/15 7:45 PM

Bryan Warner
@BryanWarner775   ☼   ⚲ Follow

#PlannedParenthood shooter has done more in one day to save black babies, then #BlackLivesMatter has done in the last several months.

RETWEETS   LIKES
9   7

5:46 PM - 27 Nov 2015

Personally speaking, I do not agree with many of the stances of Planned Parenthood, especially its Margaret Sanger eugenics origins and Negro [birth control] Project. At the same time I've partnered with this organization on various occasions to help provide some positive abstinence education programs/services for teens within my city who live in a county where the teenage pregnancy and STD rates are among the highest in New York State. NO these programs/services weren't promoting abortion to young black females or sterilization to young black males, they were geared towards educating our youth about making healthy, responsible choices. You may not agree with abortion and that's understandable. At the same time it should also be understandable that our youth need access to programs/services to teach them how to make healthy, responsible choices with their bodies, with others bodies and how they use social media especially concerning the dangers of sext messaging.

As a black man, I live in a society where anything I say or do will be used against me inside of a court of law, outside of a court of law and in the court of public opinion via the mainstream media, if I'm allowed to live. If you are a person of color, you are in the same position. People like James Holmes, Michael Dunn, Robert Lewis Dear and others can commit horrifying acts yet are not judged by the same standard and are often allowed to live to see their first court appearance. They are the monstrous face of the psychopathic and sociopathic backdrop the dominant society does not want to take responsibility for. I've said it before and I'll say it again in regards to controlling the narrative: we must create, protect and perpetuate our own media platforms to make sure we lay this responsibility in their lap. We can't wait on a benevolent mainstream media to unmask these murderers, we must do it ourselves. We can't wait to see if they're going to call it what it is, we must call it what it is: White Domestic Terrorism. The world needs to know that there's much truth to the American Horror Film genre and characters like Jason Voorhees, Norman Bates, Damien Thorn [The Omen], Jack Torrence [The Shining] and Michael Myers aren't just made up from someone's sick imagination. There are real people we've lived amongst, for generations, who've committed horrific terrorist acts of violence that make these character's films look Rated G. They're not Muslims, nor are they black/brown people. They're American males, often self described Christians, who are White Domestic Terrorists.

Esteem

An important part of building our children's self esteem is informing them about their actual ancestors [family members] who did great things. Teaching them about their great-grandparents who were successful business owners, an aunt who published books of poetry, the cousin who taught himself to play multiple instruments by ear, the great great-grandfather who was a Senator, the great aunt who was the first woman to earn a degree at a certain college and etc. shows our children their unlimited possibilities and infinite potential. Not only are they a composite of these ideas and accomplishments, they are the living expectation of greatness!

Some of our children don't know their capabilities because they don't know what their family has actually contributed to this world. Make that unknown known by teaching them about the legacy they are entrusted with. A legacy they must preserve and perpetuate.

Congruence

In the wilderness, the philosophy, That's 'MY' understanding" and "That's 'YOUR' understanding" will get somebody killed... Especially when you can't agree on what kind of snake that is sitting in the middle of the path or which berries are actually safe to eat!

Francophobia
The France Attacks and American Amnesia

On Friday November 13th in France over 120 people died from attacks carried out at six separate sites. The largest number of death tolls occurred at a concert hall during the set of American rock band the Eagles of Death Metal. Like the Kenyan school shooting this past April where 147 people lost their lives, the September Borno State Bombings in Nigeria that killed over 145 people, the over 500 people who died in South India from heat waves last May and approximately 1,000 citizens, about 3 people per day mostly people of color, who have already been killed by law enforcement this year in America, all of us should be aware of how precious all human life is. However, this is not always the case. Sometimes people simply view the lost of one life differently then the lost of another life, the deaths of one group of people more important than the deaths of another group of people.

Following the #FranceAttacks I saw many people immediately show their support and solidarity with the French people by sending out prayers and changing their Facebook Profile pictures to the France Flag via a social media option/initiative spearheaded by Facebook founder Mark Zukerberg and the encouragement of an American outcry for Americans to stand with France. Youtube even changed its logo to the French Flag and announced "We stand with Paris" on their home page. Some people just followed that script. For others it wasn't because an American battery was put in their back; they simply spoke out and showed their solidarity like they do wherever tragedy occurs on the planet. Whether these people were the former or later, it still shows that people have some sense of global consciousness simply because we're aware. We also need to be aware that things aren't always what they appear to be, especially when you look at the historical way America has interacted with France. Now that many of you are thinking globally and considering France and America, let me share a few things with you to give you.

Do you remember France opposed the invasion of Iraq and Congress changed their cafeteria menus to stop calling french fries "French" fries, started calling them "Freedom" fries?

Then the American government started encouraging Americans to call them freedom fries too? Yeah, I know it's petty. It also shows how soon some of us forget such petty things. Does that sound like an ally? See, through the lens of colonialism, your allies or enemies is based upon your geopolitical agenda and socioeconomic interests. In other words, the ends justify the means. Some people are genuinely concerned about the tragedy that happened in France, other places around the world and the tragedies that happen in America. Some people just see tragedy as an opportunity.

Speaking of allies and enemies, let me break something else down to you about the dysfunctional relationship between America and France most people don't talk about. France was the first country to accept women into freemasonry. You know, "Freemasonry", the sausage party secret society many of America's Founding Fathers, signers of the Declaration of Independence, Presidents, Congressmen, Mayors, Senators, Councilmen, Soldiers, Businessmen, Police Chiefs, Sheriffs, School Principals, Union Leaders, Judges, Newspaper Editors, Lawyers and other 'men' in positions of power belong to in this society?

Maria Deraismes: The First Female Freemason

From the 1700s to this day, the United Grand Lodge of England (UGLE), other mainstream Lodges and Prince Hall Lodges in North America still don't let women join. Any lodge, particularly French and Continental Lodges, who admit women are considered bogus by mainstream North American, Grand and Prince Hall Lodges who only have seperate associated [auxillary] bodies women can join. If you, male or female, have been initiated into a French Lodge or attend them you're generally marked as clandestine [bogus] and shunned by other freemasons. Keep in mind that these are the same marked/shunned French freemasons who are afiliated with the Grand Orient Temple who created and gifted an original Statue of Liberty to America that was initially rejected because she was black.

Now what does this have to do with the price of tea in China? Well the same way you have influential people socially engineering events that were/are Freemasons here in America, you have the same influential people socially engineering events that were/are Freemasons in France. They historically haven't, and generally don't, rock with eachother. Behind the veil of so-called alliances there are fundamental masonic differences between America and France as it relates to their geopolitical agendas and socioeconomic interests. Some of the historical pettiness, jeering and criticism Americans have about France being weak and bogus is really based upon how American Freemasons have generally looked at and still look at the French for allowing women into the lodge. Because of that, and regardless what you see on the surface, America and France have irreconcilable masonic differences that historical tragedies, and tragedies like we just witnessed, have not been able to mend. What looks like solidarity today will be separation with a side of sarcasm, tomorrow.

This is at the root of some of America's "Francophobia" - the historical stereotypes and hostility towards the French government, culture and people of France. And no, I didn't make that word up. Research it.

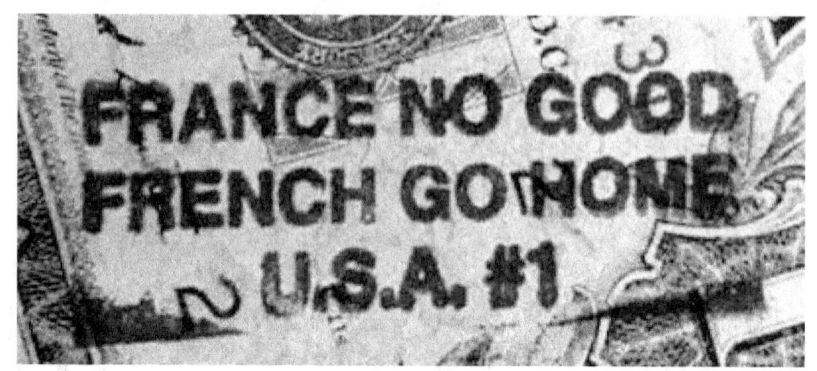

Francophobia

In closing, I think it's important to speak out against tragedies wherever and whenever they happen to human beings. All of us should. Yet we shouldn't allow ourselves to be used as a patriotic tool, especially in the midst of tragedies, to blindly support the political agendas of some people who obviously don't feel the same way about all human lives based upon their domestic and foreign policy record. Acknowledging and mourning the loss of human life, especially in great numbers such as the Native American and Armenian Genocide, the Trans-Atlantic Slave Trade and the Holocaust, is likewise important. Yet we also must know whom we are mourning with. Like in the film American Gangster when Bumpy Johnson died, sometimes people show up at a family's funeral, speak empty condolences and even sit around and eat up the family's food at the repast [repass] knowing they didn't really like the person who died, or their family. In fact, they probably had a bunch of sh*t to say about them the day before that family's tragedy. This is how some Americans responded to the death of not only the French who lost their lives but also Kenyans, Nigerians, South Indians and even other American citizens who are people of color. I just want those of you who are riding the American solidarity with France wave to clearly understand that after the water subside, America will return to biting France's back out just like sports analysts and everyday talking heads do LeBron James. And I hope to see your solidarity against that petty hypocrisy, too.

In-For-mation

When it's said that we are in the Information Age that's exactly what it means: The in-form-ation Age. Society doesn't genuinely invest in creativity, art, innovation or originality. If it appears so, it's only to replicate it for profit and/or to militarize it. People are socialized to get and stay "in formation." Discover your purpose! Be yourself! Break the mold! Make your contribution to this world to insure that our children have access to a better place than when you arrived here.

Justice or Else
What's Next?
7 Experiences of a Five Percenter

It's 3:09am and I'm up reflecting and writing on the 10.10.15 Justice or Else Rally in Washington DC I recently attended. Although there were many things I saw and heard, here are 7 Experiences I wanted to share with all of you. Before I do that I want to first give a shout out and thank my brother Keith Muhammad of Luv4Self for organizing our trip and the other members of our entourage for travelling down.

- I loved seeing the numerous vendors utilizing this entrepreneurship opportunity to provide goods/services for the people. It was definitely an example of cooperative economics. Aside from the economic stimulus to the city's economy via food, lodging, transportation and etc., I'm already working on something to address and redirect some of that revenue to neglected communities/commercial zones when gatherings like this take place, regardless of the City/State.

- The "Justice or Else: What's Next?" National Community Forum I participated in focused on various grassroot programs, projects and initiatives we're engaged in that already addresses "What's Next?" We discussed the political process, displacement/gentrification, education models, cooperative economics and etc. The best part about grassroot forums such as this is people don't simply leave encouraged. We were there working and we left with tasks. For example, during a segment we took a moment to come up with a vision statement and #hashtags to start tweeting a public official to begin using our social networks to mobilize around a specific quality of life issue. Click the highlighted link so you can check it out.

"Justice or Else: What's Next" National Community Forum

- I'm glad I had an opportunity to connect with so many people in the flesh who are working towards bringing about a better world for our present and future generations. I'm also glad that I was able to connect with my Queens and Howard University students Asiyah and Aziza and share some time with my eldest Asiyah because her 20th Born Day was also 10.10.15. In addition, 10.10.15 marks the 51st year and formal Born Day of the Five Percenters so it was also beautiful to celebrate that with some of my Universal Family. One of my best highlights was finally meeting the young sun my God Brother and his Queen gave me the honor of naming "Khemel." That was indeed love to the highest degree!

- By the time I arrived in DC I was running on fumes: the last full meal I had was a day earlier and I hadn't slept in 60 hours. Although I ended up eating some of the food/water donated by Author D. Scott I still hadn't slept taking turns driving back. Not sure if any of you have experienced this before but lack of sleep can make you hallucinate. At one point the white vehicle in front of me turned red and looked like a Dumb & Dumber version of Clifford The Big Red Dog. Lol I say this to say: when you're travelling, make sure you get some rest first and possibly when you arrive somewhere, before you travel back.

- Of the many positive things people said to me, one of the things that struck me was a brother saying how proud he was of me for the way I represent Five Percenters worldwide. It wasn't a back handed compliment and he was sincere about it. I appreciated that because it's not often that brothers put their EGO aside and honestly give another brother credit like that without wrapping it up in joke or mumbling it. Herein lies a greater problem with that mentality: When we're not sharing our love, support and appreciation for each other, we're not showing our younger generations how to love, support and appreciate each other. One of the reasons we don't see it in our millennial generation is because they don't see us doing it. I've not had an issue sharing love, support and appreciation for what others are doing and willfully that gesture symbolizes a growing sense of unity and cooperation we need as brothers to effectively address the problems that are plaguing our families and communities.

- The "or Else" means many things to many people. To me it's an unfinished sentence that represents the consequences of apathy, disunity, egotism and blind consumerism. So for example, "Justice or else... we're going to see the continual deterioration of our families and communities." Sometimes in order to build, some things must be destroyed. In this case, and among other things, it's apathy, disunity, egotism and blind consumerism that must be destroyed in order to transform our present conditions.

- If we're participating in a nationwide blackout/boycott to not support certain businesses and services we also should blackout/boycott promoting and advertising certain businesses and services. For example, not buying Polo gear for a couple of days yet simultaneously posting pictures on Instagram, Twitter and/or Facebook wearing Polo gear defeats the purpose of participating in a blackout/boycott. Even though we didn't buy anything, we may have encouraged half a dozen people to go buy something. Lol Just something to think about. Here's a video I did entitled Advertising and Self Determination where I further elaborate on this.

In closing I had an excellent time building and networking with others, seeing the beauty of our unity and leaving with more ideas to continue my work at home and abroad.

Regardless who was there, who spoke and etc., people will ultimately take away from this event what they brought to it and willfully what they gained while being there. The above video visually documents part of my experience there. The background music is a track called "Pressure" which was also produced by me.

Parental Advice

Adults, if you're ever feeling down, pessimistic, discouraged or not hopeful about what the future will bring, go invest some quality time with our youth. They will show/teach you there's something to live for and more to look forward to in life.

In Regards to Veteran's Day

I would like to take a moment to recognize all of those men and women who have sacrificed their lives as enlisted members of this country's armed forces. I also will that one day this country genuinely reciprocates that recognition across the board, beyond the celebration of a day. How? By supporting legislation and initiatives for fair Veteran and Veteran Family services/benefits that many have come home to fight for, some have even died for, right here on U.S. soil.

Veterans are a marginalized group within this society and they deserve more than a thank-you, a salute or a free Starbucks coffee. As civilians, I encourage you to learn more about the challenges they face and how you can be of any assistance via NABVETS, NOVA, other Veteran advocate organizations, your local VA Hospital and even just talking to your family members who are Veterans.

Surviving versus Thriving

Went to a Youth Forum this morning about how to deal with the police. A lawyer/former state trooper and retired buffalo police officer shared some valuable information on what to do, what not to do and how to "survive" these situations to live another day. One of the things I emphasized is that while providing our youth with the skills to survive, our focus must be on the end game; their need to THRIVE.

The movement in Ferguson that has gained momentum around the world is primarily youth driven because they/we are frustrated, angry and dissatisfied with surviving. We've accepted enough! To many of us, being told to just do what's required in order to make it home alive sounds like we need to accept it and go along with the way things are; "just be happy you're alive." Many of us want to thrive. Our ability to thrive includes survival, yet hinges upon channeling our frustration, anger and dissatisfaction to establish a different status quo. Our youth need to know, and it must be emphasized, that self determination is our end game.

Ujamaa

Ujamaa means 'Cooperative Economics': To build and maintain our own stores and other businesses and to profit from them together. It's our willingness, ability and commitment to get money together in a positive way, for the good of our communities.

In order to establish, support and grow strong businesses and a local economy we all benefit from, we must find cooperative ways to eat together. If not, competitive conditions are created where people begin to feed off of each other. Ujamaa encourages us to share a seat at a table we prepare, not become the main course on someone else's menu.

Setting Goals

A long-term goal is a series of successful short-term goals.

Minister Louis Farrakhan
Friend Or Foe?

One week following the 10.10.15 Justice or Else Rally in Washington, DC I couldn't help but notice the widespread criticism of Minister Farrakhan and his Nation of Islam by both mainstream media and the everyday person via their social media page. Some of these criticisms have been outright name calling such as "FarraCON" or 'FarraCoon"; defining the minister as a misleading charlatan that's blood sucking the poor. Others have been less abrasive and have articulated their desire to see the evidence and practical application of "or Else" -which they claim wasn't defined at the rally. In his defense, some of his supporters have retorted that a General doesn't announce his strategies to the public, the minister has laid out plans of action years before the rally and people have no right to question someone in his position because they're not the leader. Well today I wanted to offer a perspective to willfully help reconcile these perspectives.

For those who are Anti-Farrakhan:

First and foremost, I think it's important to keep in mind that as a leader, some view the minister as a spiritual father, father figure and ultimately someone who occupies a parental role within their life. Considering this, whatever your criticisms are of him, it sounds and feels no different than you talking about someone's parent. Imagine someone talking about your mother or father. Regardless how respectful or on point someone is with a criticism of your parent, you're going to feel some kind of way about it, initially. I don't know many people who are comfortable with someone calling their parent names, ridiculing them or etc.: those are usually fighting words. Even though no person, parent or not, is above criticism, there's always a certain level of respect we've shown our parents even if they were dead wrong. And when I say respect I don't mean "agree and go along with any and everything they say" because sometimes they're not the best knower in every given life situation. To take it a step further: even though the minister may not look it and he colors his hair, he is an eighty-two-year old grandparent and great-grandparent. That in itself warrants the kind of respect we show any elder, not just a parent. And just like our own grandparents and great-grandparents, we may not agree with everything they're saying or doing, but out of respect, there's a way we should talk to and talk about them. That is the posture, decorum and etiquette of a civilized person.

Because I am a free thinker I don't agree with what everyone says or does. Everyone doesn't always agree with me and there are times I reassess something I said or did and don't agree with myself. That being said, I think it's healthy to express the right to critically analyze what anyone says or does. However, I think we have that right not simply for the purpose of argument or to point out what we think is wrong. We have that right, and responsibility, to show and prove what's wrong by presenting what's right. In other words, if you think I can use a better strategy in my STYA Program to teach my youth, don't just point out what you think I'm doing wrong, offer me the right way. When you approach people by penalizing them, as opposed to offering them an alternative, people tend to shut down and be unreceptive to what you have to say. For example, I also teach preschool in addition to my program and there are times I see my students do something wrong. One day I gave some students instructions on practicing their writing. When I walked over to check their work they weren't following the instructions. They were writing, they just weren't following the right instructions. I didn't walk over, snatch the pencil out of their hand and say,

"No, that's not how you do it. This is the right way." I said, acknowledging they were at least writing, "Hey…, that's good. Now see if you can write it this way" as a patted them on the shoulder and redirected them back to the right instructions. As adults the same approach, sense of consideration and tact applies. People are generally more welcoming to being offered alternatives than just being criticized or even ridiculed for what they feel, think or believe. This is not to say that we should not engage in intellectual discourses and tiptoe around everybody. This is to say that the basis of these discourses should not be for the purpose of name calling, to ridicule others or for pissing contests. The purpose of any intellectual discourse, especially with our people, should be to discuss and assess the best ideas and strategies to solve our problems. If someone is so caught up in their feelings that they have an inability to rise above their emotions for that purpose, then you need to walk away. Some people worship who they perceive as their leaders, whether it's Jesus, Muhammad, Beyonce, Buddha, Minister Farrakhan and even The Father Allah. And anything you have critical to say about them will be outright rejected, including you and some of your well meaning uninvolved associates.

For those who are Pro-Farrakhan:

Just because someone questions a man or woman's idea or strategy it doesn't make them an agent, hypocrite, hater or anything else some of you define as antagonistic. Sometimes people simply have and can share a perspective others don't see. This is the reason Minister Farrakhan has a research team; there are things he simply doesn't know or understand and he relies on a counsel of advisors to teach him. And yes, some of them are about half of his age. Now keep in mind that there are many people who are not a part of the minister's advisor team who are more than qualified to advise him, and them, too. Many of these men and women are not Muslims nor are they registered members of his Nation of Islam. Some of them are a part of your social networks and you interact with them often. I mention this to emphasize the fact that knowledge is inexhaustible which gives everyone the potential of being a best knower in any given situation. Some find it difficult to grasp this reality because it seems to conflict with a hierarchal structure of having one leader at the top and a descending order of roles beneath them. It's difficult to imagine that someone beneath the person at the top can conceptualize something beyond that leader's realm of thinking. It's also difficult to imagine that the person at the top cannot conceptualize something from someone that's beneath them. You are aware that someone had to teach Minister Farrakhan how to set up and use a Twitter account right? I'm sure you also know his team of advisors put him on to certain Rappers he never heard about before because they were key support contacts he needed to meet in order to promote the Justice or Else rally, right? The point in saying this is to remind all of you that the title of leader doesn't mean that someone personally has all of the answers. No great leader would make that claim, and when these leaders do make the honest claim that it's not about them, and even give credit to their benefactors, many of us simply don't believe it.

One of the other things that's important to understand is this: there are those who respectfully disagree with the 10.10.15 Justice or Else rally because they have a hard time "quantifying" it. Sure many can speak about the quality of their personal experience and no one can take that away from them, but how do you accurately quantify or measure that experience? This is one of the reasons some people were/are discouraged and disenchanted with the rally; they don't see a tangible, concrete example of "What's next?" For example, the 2015 BET Hip Hop Awards viewer ratings were down over 50% [1.4 million] this year from 2014. It can be argued that this plunge is a direct result of the BET Boycott social media campaign against the network for not covering the rally. You can even argue how the current nationally conscious #BlackLivesMatter backdrop, coupled with the Justice or Else rally, has created the Anti-Empire sentiments responsible for their weekly rating drop. That is quantifiable, it's tangible and concrete. For those who would like to effectively demonstrate the rally's impact, or even the minister's impact on a local, regional, national or international level, these kinds of quantifiable Talking Points are necessary to show and prove it. Some people are simply not moved by someone's personal beliefs or human interest stories. Understandably, some people want to know what's in it for them, what is the actual outcome, if/when they invest their time and/or money into something.

In conclusion, I think it's important to keep the focus on the collective movement of people who are actually invested in programs, projects and initiatives to bring about justice. I had an opportunity to participate in a National Community Forum after the rally which echoes these sentiments. It took place at We Act Radio Station [Washington DC] and its purpose was to bring people from across the nation together to discuss these programs, projects and initiatives we're already invested in and how you can also get involved. In addition to checking out the above link for ideas of how you can get involved, here is something else you can do and share with others: Down from 11% last season, we the people are again calling for a Nationwide Boycott during the Holiday season (November – December) to not purchase any goods or services. If anyone makes any purchases, it should be strictly with Black-owned businesses. Also, we are encouraging everyone to not advertise or promote any goods, services, brands/logos of outside companies using their social networks [Instagram, Facebook, Twitter and etc.]. We should only advertise or promote Black-owned businesses. Let's keep our personal beefs and religious disagreements off of social media and at home. Publically we must continue to be positively invested in this collective momentum that's quantifying the transformation we would like to see.

Ujima

Ujima means 'Collective Work and Responsibility'; building/maintaining our community, solving our problems together and sharing in our successes and accomplishments. Some people are all about themselves until they find themselves in a situation. Then we realize the value of being responsible for one another and working collectively. Many times our very life, and the lives of our loved ones, depend upon that realization.

The more we are there [for each other], we minimize situations that appear to come out of nowhere. We need each other.

Kujichagulia

Kujichagulia means 'Self-Determination' and the importance of defining, naming, creating and speaking for ourselves. Amongst other things, our sense of identity and purpose requires heart; the love and resilience to be. And it is with heart, that we determine the shape of our destiny. So be, great!

Chickens coming home to roost

Some people are implying or saying that the lives of the NY Police Officers who were murdered don't matter because they wore a blue uniform, regardless if they were good people. I wonder if something were to happen to their family/children because of the black uniform they're born in, regardless if they were good people, would they expect the same careless response from people. It's something to think about. Also, those chickens people talk about that come home to roost..., lay eggs.

The Unstoppable

One key to being unstoppable is to stop telling people what you're going to do. Show them after you're done.

A Quest For Fire!

It's a stretch to even find slang or colloquialisms used by our present generation that doesn't communicate fire and a fearless desire for self determination. "Turnt Up", "Get It Poppin'", "Hot Nigga", "0 to 100" and etc. all reflect a latent revolutionary spirit that's not going to go sit down somewhere, that doesn't worship a white jesus and won't beg somebody for peace. That energy must be acknowledged, embraced and rightly guided.

MOST Black Men...

One of the surest ways to get blindsided by life is to start off with a wrong or false premise. A premise is the basis [foundation] of an argument or theory. For example, if I start off saying "MOST women...", that is the wrong premise to argue from. It suggests that I know most women when I absolutely don't. Therefore, everything that concludes that wrong statement has more of a chance to be wrong too. Why? The foundation isn't solid. If you've ever witnessed a person start off with the wrong premise you may have also seen that conversation take a sharp detour to address the wrong premise before going any further. For example, before I could even go into talking about "MOST women" a critical thinker would first address the fact that I don't know most women to speak on them. Starting off wrong sets the tone for whatever else I have to say about women that has a high probability of being wrong too. At best, all I could say is "most women I know" -which sets the right premise and frames the conversation in the proper context.

What inspired this article are the countless false premises and arguments I see offline and on social media. While some false premises are deliberately made as clickbait, there are those who simply don't know how to soundly communicate their ideas. They may be well intended, and even have a valid point to make about their own personal experiences or observations, yet it all goes out of the window when they start wrong. I once saw a Facebook post get so out of hand that it resulted in violence offline, all because of a wrong premise about how someone died.

I recently had an online exchange with a black woman who shared a post of a white man being interviewed by a black woman on a South African News Station. Out of frustration of her questions, the white man walked off of the show and threatened her to the point he had to be escorted out of the building. The woman who posted this video captioned it, *"This is how most black men treat black women now a days. It's pitiful"* Upon seeing this I commented that at best all she could accurately say is, *"most black men I know."* Instead of considering the fundamental flaw in her statement her only response was *"My mother always told me only a hit dog makes noise.*" The irony in this is she was literally talking to a black man who is not "MOST black men" she described. In fact, all of my colleagues are not like that. When faced with this scenario some people take pride in trying to convince someone like this otherwise. If it's a child who lacks the experience then I share with them some examples they can consider outside of their sphere of awareness. If it's an adult with no physical/mental impairments that limits their experience or sphere of awareness then I don't waste time trying to explain anything. This is an able-bodied adult who is ignorant by choice. Meaning, they choose to ignore new information and experience anything outside of their limited sphere of awareness. With this person it is only a matter of time before life shows them something otherwise. In this woman's case, who was single, she'll miss brothers like myself who don't fit into her conceptual prison house.

As I said, many arguments start from the place of a wrong premise. Consider Donald Trump's false premise about Mexican Immigrants that, *"THEY [The Mexican Government] send the bad ones over because they don't want to pay for them"* or Hillary Clinton's 1996 Speech at Keene State College Speech describing inner-city [black and brown] youth as *"superpredators"* -a word first mentioned by Princeton Political Science Professor John DiIulio to describe these youth as subhuman, wild, amoral creatures ready to violate and murder Americans without a conscience. Both of these false premises, and many others, have been used to criminalize people of color in this country and reinforce an image of inferiority/distrust that permeates every institution, that colors every resource and fuels this economy.

How do we begin to change that? To start, knowledge must be our foundation, not belief, hearsay or feelings. Having the facts enables us to speak from a position of surety and confidence because our proposition is sound. When we start off right, with the right information, the conclusions drawn from what we say and do will be less likely to be wrong. Belief, hearsay and feelings don't afford us the same sense of security and stability because they aren't concrete. People believe whatever they want regardless of the facts, hearsay is nothing but a rumor and feelings change like the wind. While there's a place for all of these perspectives, they're not the most sound sources to build upon because they're too transitory [impermanent]. The more we know, we have the ability to make wiser decisions. It's difficult to make wise decisions when we don't know anything first. So as we become more informed about people, places and things, we'll begin to expand our sphere of awareness and experience life beyond the limits of belief, hearsay and feelings. We'll begin to "know" the "ledge" [knowledge] of the false premises we once stood upon and willfully speak and act wiser than we did before.

In the series Kung Fu, Master Kan in speaking to his student Caine about perceiving the way of nature said, "*Avoid rather than check. Check rather than hurt. Hurt rather than maim. Maim rather than kill. For all life is precious nor can any be replaced.*" With growth and development comes power. This influence makes us a resource and responsible to those who are unaware. There are times I didn't follow the above advice in regards to mental combat and killed rather than maim, maimed instead of checking a person and checked a person instead of avoiding them. As I've gotten older I realize that many arguments can be avoided with a few well chosen words or avoiding the conversation altogether in order to preserve the relationship. People are capable of drawing the right conclusions, such as "my love wasn't wrong, I just shared it with a person unwilling to reciprocate it" if they can get their premise right, "there is a chance for love" as opposed to a false premise like "b*tches ain't sh*t but hoes and tricks" or "all men cheat." It takes courage and receptivity to think outside of the box before stepping outside of the box, but it's a way of thinking and a step that's worth it. To say that MOST or ALL people, places and things are a certain way, especially when we don't know MOST or ALL people, places and things, is equivalent to building a house with straw or sticks. And it's only a matter of time before the big bad wolf comes and huffs, puffs and blows that house down.

Empty Advice

Criticisms are best made with our contribution(s). It's better to give a person something with our advice.

Boys To Men

Boys who don't learn the value of a woman often become men looking for ass instead of empaths.

Sep 9, 2016 4:39pm

It's not about ideas, it's about our execution.

Poor Righteous Teachers

"Poor Righteous Teachers" are righteous teachers whose primary target audience are the poor, underserved and disenfranchised -even though we teach everybody. If we were in Old Europe we would be Serf Righteous Teachers. That phrase doesn't mean to be broke, busted, disgusted or impoverished trying to teach people what's right.

5 Ways To Keep Luke Cage Relevant

The new hit show Luke Cage literally broke Netflix last week and some are wondering if it's a fluke or will it remain relevant.

As a youth advocate and preschool teacher from Generation X, I was born between 1961-1979, there are many things I learn from and teach our Millennials [Generation Y],

Generation Z and Generation Alpha I primarily interact with everyday. Born between the years 1980-1995, 1996-2010 and 2011-2025, these are the generations who represent the Ambassadors of our future and what they know and understand will be the infrastructure and decorum of that future. It's important to mention this because we often overlook the fact that they will one day be in charge of social security, senior citizen housing and any legislation that will directly effect us as their elders. It's not only important to consider what they think but be involved in their growth and development.

Anyway, prior to this Marvel Television web series release I've kept up with the comic book narrative of Luke Cage with hopes of seeing "Power Man" on the big screen. The day came, the internet went batshit crazy and review after review heralded this superhuman Harlemite with unbreakable skin as the crime fighting [Black] God the Five Percenters have identified themselves as since 1964. Among its detractors were some white folks crying about the Harlem backdrop not being a gentrified North Manhattan and Wendy Williams posted a picture of Mike Colter [Luke Cage] with his white wife during an interview to discredit his Marvel Universe archetype, in real life. While people have been debating the social impact and relevance of this web series, many have failed to ask our Millennials and Generation Z what they think. I have been. I've also been checking out their commentary and reviews of Luke Cage and what I've found is they generally don't care or know enough of the social/cultural context to actually appreciate it. To many of them it's more of a novelty, not a statement of sociopolitical consciousness. For example, unless children born between 1980 and 2010 have Generation X or Baby Boomer parents and grandparents schooling them about the past, they'll have no idea what "70s Blaxploitation" is -which Luke Cage has been touted as. Of course there are exceptions, but even the best of Millennials and Generation Z who claim Hip Hop have no clue where episode names like "Who's Gonna Take The Weight?", "Manifest" or "DWYCK" came from. In mass, those who seem to appreciate this web series the most are my generation, Generation X, and some of the Baby Boomers.

The beauty in this is I've found myself challenged to introduce our youth to a deeper perspective and appreciation for where they are and what they have in Luke Cage, especially in a time where we are seeing un-human black men with breakable skin being murdered by police every day. From this introspection and experience I came up with 5 ways we can help build upon this narrative so our youth can get the most out of this web series and what's happening around it. These are 5 things I encourage you to consider if you're invested in doing the same:

1.) Watch the web series, encourage our youth to watch it and watch it with them if you can. Invest in the web series when it's available and keep it in your digital library.

2.) Have open discussions that include Luke Cage within the Marvel Universe conversation alongside other super heroes/sheroes. Contrast and compare his ability to others. This morning in my preschool class I began teaching one of my 4 year old boys about Luke Cage, AKA "Power Man", by showing him who he was on my computer. When comparing him to Superman he said he needs a cape to which I simply responded, "He doesn't even need one, he looks and dresses just like you."

3.) Research social/cultural themes that are expressed or implied within the web series. For example, every episode is named after a Gang Starr song and this is an excellent opportunity to share their contribution to Hip Hop.

4.) Support positive products/services that reinforce these themes within the web series.

5.) If you celebrate Halloween, encourage the youth to dress like one of the web series characters and/or dress like one of these characters yourself along with them. How cool would it be as a Father to be Luke Cage? If you celebrate Christmas, support products, especially from black owned businesses, that reinforce the themes within the web series.

The ultimate goal here is to own, control and build upon this narrative. In regards to identity, it's important to orientate ourselves with language, symbols and archetypes of empowerment, especially in a society that promotes white nationalism, supremacy and iconography. It's also important to seek out and support black comic book writers, graphic designers and etc. Unlike our past generations, today our Millennials [Generation Y], Generation Z and Generation Alpha have the benefit of knowing and identifying with a Storm, Black Panther, The Falcon, Deadshot and now Luke Cage. We must take advantage of these opportunities. More importantly, we must create our own. Lastly, we need more positive images in real life, real men and women of power who are fighting crime and setting a righteous standard so that our families don't have to live in fear. This doesn't require us to gain superpowers in a sabotaged cellular regeneration experiment. It requires care and commitment to our people.

Youth Health & Wellness

Every morning my preschoolers do physical exercises and breathing exercises to promote optimum health, coordination and self-regulation. I also encourage them to make up exercises such as this stretch one of them came up with. By incorporating their own ideas they also have a voice and sense of ownership in the process and the purpose of the project.

This image of Jesus and the Disciples was found in the Catacombs of Domitilla, Rome [Italy] in 400 AD. It's one of the oldest if not the oldest image depicting him. And no that ain't smoke or dirt making their color look black or smeared paint making it look like they got afros.

Conspiracy Theorists Guide to The Birth of a Nation

Before I saw The Birth of a Nation I, like many of you, have been bombarded with controversy surrounding this film. Unlike the original 1915 American silent film The Birth of a Nation (The Clansman) that revered the KKK and was screened at the White House, this version by Nate Parker focuses on the life of Rev. Nat Turner and his slave revolt that took place in 1831 in Southampton County, Virginia. From two-faced people who praised The Great Debaters now crucifying Nate Parker about a decades old rape allegation, to people critiquing its weekend box office numbers like its a rap album trying to go platinum. From black feminists who didn't see the film debating about scenes that didn't exist, to white folks writing bruised ego reviews because they looked bad. Everybody and their dog has had something to say about this film that has evoking many people to feel some kinda way. Many reviews have been calling it a strait box office flop. My question is, how Sway? How? To begin, this was a $100,000 personal investment for Parker. That's how much he put up. The rest of the $8.5 million production budget was made possible by other investors. Premiering at the 2016 Sundance Film Festival, the largest U.S. independent festival which annually takes place in Utah, The Birth of a Nation was honored as the Best of the Fest and won the Audience Award of a U.S. Drama and the U.S. Grand Jury Prize. To get this kind of reception at this festival is BIG! It was so big that following its premiere Fox Searchlight Pictures, The Weinstein Company, Sony Pictures Entertainment and Netflix got in a bidding war to buy it. That doesn't look like a lemon to me. Parker eventually sold its "worldwide rights" to Fox Searchlight Pictures for an unprecedented $17.5 million. Remember, this was a $100,000 personal investment for Parker. When the film was finally released in 2,105 theaters across America on October 7th, the opening weekend brought in $7 million. At the date of this writing, the film has grossed $15 million; a $6.5 million profit when you subtract the $8.5 million production budget. The only way to describe that is profitable and this profit is not even considering its Lifetime Gross potential. For example, The Color Purple had a budget of $15 million and in a generation has grossed $98.4 million to date. Naw The Birth of a Nation didn't have no $245 million production budget like Star Wars: The Force Awakens, a package that was flipped almost 9 times since December 2015 to reach $2 billion worldwide, but The Birth of a Nation is still a profitable investment that will appreciate in value over time. It's modest slow money.

One of the main criticisms surrounding this film, that has been levied at Nate Parker, has been some 1999 rape charges Parker was acquitted for in 2001. I cannot say for sure what went down yet the court transcripts can offer those of you some insight. What I will say is that black actresses, actors, producers, directors and etc. are treated very different in Hollywood and in the Media. For example, take white writer, actor and Oscar-winning director Roman Polanski who was arrested and charged in 1977 for rape by use of drugs, perversion, sodomy, lewd and lascivious act upon a child under 14, and furnishing a controlled substance to a minor. Polanski took a plea deal of a lesser charge of engaging in unlawful sexual intercourse but before the sentencing he fled to France and has been living as a fugitive ever since. Now living in Poland, its Prime Minister Zbigniew Ziobro has recently called upon its Supreme Court to extradite Polanski to the US. Here's the kicker, over 100 Hollywood directors have stepped up in the past, even signing a petition, to show their support for Polanski while well aware of his plea deal. One of those supporters, another writer, actor and Academy Award-winning director Woody Allen who actually married his step daughter who was thirty-five years younger than him, has also been accused of molesting a 7 year old child. I mention this to give context to a double standard. At this very moment Roman Polanski and Woody Allen are still praised, awarded and looked upon as Hollywood Icons yet people aren't really talking about how pervasive this sickness is in America, including women rights activists and feminists. I did back in January when the Bill Cosby accusations came out. All things being equal, I would love to see a larger discussion about men like Polanski, Allen, other men and women like them, and even boycotts of their films -especially from those who are leading these critiques about Nate Parker's accusations.

Falls woman ties roots to original 'Uncle Tom'

By SUSAN MIKULA CAMPBELL
Niagara Gazette

Inez Dorsey Frank, 78, of Niagara Falls, didn't know until about eight years ago that she was related to one of the more famous passengers on the Underground Railroad.

A cousin told her that she is a great-granddaughter of the Rev. Josiah Henson, believed to be the model for Uncle Tom in Harriet Beecher Stowe's 19th century anti-slavery novel, "Uncle Tom's Cabin."

"It's something that people didn't seem to talk about. Now a lot of people are trying to find out about the roots of their family," Mrs. Frank said.

Henson was born a slave near Port Tobacco, Md. His father was taken from the family and sold. Henson also was sold away from his mother but they were later reunited.

He was ordained as a preacher by the Methodist Episcopal Church in 1828. In 1830, suspecting that he was to be sold away from his wife and children, Henson escaped with them to Canada.

In 1841, he and a group of abolitionists bought 200 acres of land in Dresden, Ont., and established a school for escaped slaves called the British-American Institute. Part of the property is now a historic site. Visitors can see Henson's cabin, grave, a sawmill and other buildings and items used by the original black settlers.

In 1849, Henson was in Boston and

dictated his autobiography, "The Life of Josiah Henson, Formerly a Slave." While in that city, he met Harriet Beecher Stowe and told her of his life as a slave.

Henson's daughter settled in St. Catharines and married former slave Alice Alexander Dorsey.

Mrs. Frank moved to Niagara Falls from Canada with her mother in 1933. Mrs. Frank's cousin, the late Gertrude Dorsey of St. Catharines, mentioned their famous ancestor in conversation one day about eight years ago.

Mrs. Frank has never read "Uncle Tom's Cabin" but she visited the Dresden historic site three years ago on a trip organized by her daughter, Edith Garrison of Buffalo.

"It was quite a thrill to see," she said.

Although she said knowing she is related to Henson gives her a nice feeling, she finds more pride in being elected mother of the year by her church and the knowledge that her daughter went back to school after 20 years and is now a Buffalo teacher.

Mrs. Frank said she really hasn't experienced prejudice.

"No matter where you go, there's always some smart alecks," she said.

Mrs. Garrison hopes to organize another trip to Dresden for her mother and other family members.

"It was good to see where we came from and understand we had no reason to walk with our heads down," she said.

RON SCHIFFERLE — Niagara Gazette

Inez Frank of Niagara Falls takes pride in knowing she is a descendant of the Rev. Josiah Henson, a former slave who reportedly inspired the central character in the novel "Uncle Tom's Cabin."

My Grandmother, Inez Dorsey Frank

In regards to the film itself, let me start by saying I appreciated it in a way that some may not be able to relate to. I am a direct descendant of prisoners of war [slaves], literally. My great-great-great grandfather Josiah Henson was born into slavery in Charles County Maryland on June 15th, 1789. A forerunner of the Underground Railroad, Henson was enslaved for 41 years until he escaped to Canada with his wife and four sons. Once settled he was instrumental in helping other blacks organize to find the land and found the Dawn Settlement through negotiating the purchase 400 acres. He was the catalyst behind establishing the British-American Institute for fugitive slaves and military strategist who organized a Black Militia who fought in the Rebellion of 1837. In addition, he continued to travel back into America many times helping hundreds gain their freedom. I was blessed to learn this as a child and it gave me a sense of pride in a legacy that many of my people didn't have the benefit of knowing. Josiah had twelve children altogether and from his family was born a great grand-nephew named Matthew Henson; a famous explorer who traveled to the North Pole that many learn about during Black History Month every year. Matthew Henson fell in love with a beautiful Inuit woman named Akatingwah and they had a son, his only child, named Anaukaq.

I mention some of my ancestry because throughout the film I couldn't help but recognize the striking parallels between the life of Josiah Henson and Nat Turner. In fact, I would not be surprised if Nate Parker used elements of my great-great-great grandfather's life for Nat Turner's narrative. Why wouldn't he? Harriet Beecher Stowe, author of one of the greatest American novels Uncle Tom's Cabin, did. Here are just some of those parallels:

➢ Both Josiah and Nathaniel are biblical names.
➢ Both were born into slavery and prophesied by elders to be great leaders among their people when they were children. This prophesy was true in both cases.
➢ Both learned scripture as children.
➢ Both of their fathers, at three or four years old, were separated from their family after assaulting a white man.
➢ Both were raised by their mothers.
➢ Both became Reverends in their late teens.
➢ Both were given permission to travel to various plantations to preach.
➢ Both were married in their early twenties.
➢ Both organized black militias to fight against oppression.

One of the most important parallels is both of these freedom fighters have been buried in American History with their names used to shield its dirt. As mentioned, elements of Josiah Henson's life were used for the novel Uncle Tom's

Cabin, yet he was no Uncle Tom. In the Pulitzer Prize-winning novel The Confessions of Nat Turner that Time Magazine included in its TIME 100 Best English-language Novels from 1923 to 2005, Nat Turner is characterized as a sex crazed bisexual simpleton. That is why it's important to share and control our narrative. If not, our future generations will think Josiah Henson was like Uncle Ruckus and Nat Turner was Ray Lewis. That is a tragedy. It's also tragic if this happened to our life when we're no longer here.

Because The Birth of a Nation is still very new I encourage you to see and judge it for yourselves. Regardless if you choose to see it or not, I also encourage you to do further research on slave revolts in North America. One of the best resource books I've read on the subject is "Black Rebellion: Eyewitness Accounts of Major Slave Revolts" by Bangladeshi author Dr. Sujan Dass.

Dec 11, 2016 8:11am

Not sure if I've ever shared this but I will. Since my childhood, whenever I'm going through a monumental change or a change is about to occur in my life I'll have a vision [dream] about school. The degree of change in my life determined the school setting; elementary, middle school, high school or college. Also, what I was doing there symbolized the type of change in my life; trying to find my locker, stressing over a specific class, organizing students or etc. This still happens to me today without fail. Well last night was one of those nights. I was travelling to enroll in a college and very excited about getting there. I was confident and comfortable with the terrain because I had been in that environment before. So I came with an expectation to share/help others with what I've learned. During the drive along the highway the grassy divider had trees and there was a mother and baby giraffe hidden amongst them. Once I arrived at the college I almost immediately connected with a woman whose love was so pure she literally moved me to tears. Not no snot bubble a** whuppin' tears, I'm talking about tears of joy. Lol She moved me, deeply! I already know part of what this means and I am receptive.

Your Vote Kinda Don't Matter, But Kinda Does, Well Let Me Explain...

This 2016 Presidential Election has been a mess. If America were a person its Face Book relationship status with the world would be 'complicated'. Every time I'm over the boarder visiting our Canadian neighbors they bring up this year's race with a somber air of condolences as if I just lost a family member. Seriously! Right now America is an international embarrassment and the world is sitting back watching what's happening in this country like it's a Monty Python marathon. I can see why so many people say they don't vote, they're not going to vote and their vote ultimately doesn't matter. Hell, I facilitate a program for adolescents and work with other youth of various ages every day and they are disgusted about what they're seeing and hearing this election and they're not even old enough to vote. So the statistical statement that Millennials are not interested in or engaged in the political process is right and exact. Because of this degree of dissatisfaction, and me having the experience as a 2013 County Legislature Candidate in my city, I'm consistently in the position to educate others about the political process. And I'm not talking about educating people based upon some "your grandmother died so you could vote", "if you don't vote you can't complain" or "your vote doesn't matter" script either. I'm talking about making the political process more accessible through breaking that sh*t down in layman's terms. In regards to terms, as in the four year term of the president, the truth is, your vote in this or any presidential election kinda doesn't matter, but kinda does, well let me explain.

The Popular Vote vs. The Electoral College Vote

When we think of voting, it's different on a local, regional and national level. When we're voting to elect local or regional public officials such as our School Board, City Council, Mayors, County Legislators, County Coroners, Senators, Assemblymen/women and etc. they get elected based upon the popular vote. in other words, we directly elect these public officials with our vote. When it comes to the national level, we are not directly electing the President and Vice-President with our popular vote. We are actually voting for representatives in our State who are then expected to vote on our behalf for the President and Vice-President we choose. These representatives are called Electors and this process is called the Electoral College. Sometimes these Electors are actually on our ballot. A lot of times they aren't on the ballot and we don't even know who the hell these people are. Electors are usually people affiliated with a Presidential candidate, state-elected officials or political party leaders. In other words, people with clout who can pull the strings, buy, bully and also destroy opponents popular voting power in order to get their own candidate elected. The Electoral College is made up of 538 Electors; a number equal to this nation's 435 Representatives, 100 Senators and 3 Electors in the District of Columbia. These 538 people are the ones who cast votes to actually decide the President and Vice-President of the United States, not the people directly. So when we go to the polls on Tuesday, we will be choosing which candidate receives our State's Electors. The candidate who gets a majority of electoral votes (270) wins the Presidency and Vice-Presidency. With the Electoral College there have been instances when a Presidential candidate won the popular vote, but lost the Electors vote. The most recent example is when Al Gore won the popular vote but the Electors said f*ck it and voted for George W Bush instead. Although this doesn't happen all of the time, the fact that it has happened and can happen again, is a problem. A fundamental problem, and flaw, in this system. To guard against this, different states have laws requiring Electors to vote for their statewide winner of the popular vote and/or sign pledges promising to support their party. In this 2016 Election we've already seen Democratic and Republican Electors step down or openly agree to break the law and accept paying a fine if they're required to vote for Hillary Clinton or Donald Trump, regardless what the popular vote is in their state to support these candidates. This is the exact kind of political atmosphere that has caused a candidate who won the popular vote, lose the Electors vote or who lost the popular vote, win the Electors vote.

So yeah, I can understand when people say their vote for the President doesn't matter but here are a few things we can actually do about it:

1.) What does matter is what we can politically control on a local and regional level, not just as voters but as lobbyists, constituents. We need to financially support the campaigns and initiatives of those candidates we want to see represent our concerns in public office. Here in New York State the Jacobs Family who owns Delaware North Companies are Governor Cuomo's best friend. Delaware North is a food, venue and management company that operates around the country in various sports arenas, state parks and etc. The Jacobs have a pretty large family during election time each family member makes a huge contribution to Cuomo's campaign. Then they make a collective donation to his campaign as a family. Because of that support, Cuomo's policies and initiatives always lean in favor of his friends, the Jacobs family. If we don't see any candidates we like, we need to financially support local organizations, businesses and community members who have initiatives that are addressing our concerns. If we don't see any of them, then we need to create something and/or look for others to create it so you can financially support that. The bottom line is we need to put money where our mouth is, especially those of us who have the most to say about what people are or aren't doing.

2.) Another vital part of local and regional control is finding out who our state Electors are, how they were vetted, holding those who gave them this position accountable and what we can do to lobby for Electors we think best represent us in the Electoral College. As Five Percenters we often talk about our ability to master city science, social science and high science. In this regard, we must ask ourselves how can we use our city science or knowledge of local and regional politics to utilize the social science or social capital to influence the higher science or politics on a national level with our Electors? An excellent example of this is the political pressure that was put on Donald Trump's Ohio campaign chair and Elector Kathy Miller for making openly racist remarks about black people during an interview with The Guardian. She resigned just hours after the interview came out.

One of my signs from my 2013 County Legislature Campaign

3.) If you want to be involved or on the fence about being involved in the political process, realize that you do have the ability to be a candidate or encourage others you would support as a candidate. It's obvious, especially on a local level, that many of the people you see on the School Board, City Council, Legislature and even your Mayor don't have any special qualifications to sit there. And yes, I mean sit there because that's what some of them are doing. You don't need no doctorates degree in political science, 10,000 hours of community service or know how to use $50 dollar words. We've had actual Presidents and Presidential candidates that are far from being people like this. So hell yeah you're qualified to represent your community, city or school district if you genuinely care about people having the proper resources and services to succeed. That's the first thing you need, heart! Heart is your moral compass that helps guide you as a candidate, and be a guide to a candidate you support, in a sea of intellectual impotence and egotistical tides of petty politricks. If you're not comfortable enough to put yourself out there as a candidate then volunteer to work on the campaign of a candidate that you support.

As I write this article we are two days away from Tuesday's General Election and what my Christian family calls The Rapture -yet neither of these political candidates are coming to save America. Those of us who live here, and plan on staying here, must save ourselves. If you're like myself, someone who doesn't support Hillary Clinton or Donald Trump, keep in mind that there are two other candidates you can research and feel good about voting for; Dr. Jill Stein of the Green Party and Gary Johnson of the Libertarian Party. If you still don't feel good after researching these candidates then I encourage you to just write-in Rev. X.

Sticks in the Mud

Don't be a stick in the mud. Be a plant in the mud.

Positive Safe-Spaces

It's important to find and go to those safe-spaces of Peace where we feel most Loved. It's equally important to build and become a safe-space of Peace where others can come and feel most Loved.

Creativity

None of us would exist without the power of creation [creativity]. So imagine trying to successfully live WITHOUT being creative. When we don't have an unrestricted, consistent, creative outlet to positively express ourselves, that stagnation only breeds sickness -and there is no amount of alcohol, drugs, recreational sex or money that can make us feel better.

Deconstructing Kanye West

Kanye West is arguably one the most creative, insightful visionaries of our time. Many would also argue that he is one of the biggest a**holes and the most immature. Whatever we think or feel about him, fifty years from now it would be virtually impossible to discuss Pop Culture during the Millennial generation without mentioning the social commentary, musical and fashion contributions of Kanye West.

Since the mid 90's of his Roc-A-Fella Producer days up to the present, West has evolved into somewhat of a Pop Cultural Messianic Figure and people either love him or hate him. Coming from an educational background in Chicago, I could always see a growing social consciousness throughout West's music and that's what resonated with me. It wasn't until September 2nd, 2005 that he took a public stance and vocally expressed it during the live Hurricane Katrina telethon by stating, "George Bush doesn't care about black people" in regards to how the government handled this natural disaster. Although he later clarified his statements, West's often unpredictable social commentary began to take center stage, often to the point of eclipsing his artistic contributions. Since 2004 to the present date West is known for his anti-Award Showism. He's done everything but storm out of, publicly criticize, boycott and even take the microphone from an artist who received an award he felt she didn't deserve. Some shows have strived to accommodate this by giving West a platform to speak and this often comes back to bite them in the a**. He's walked out in the middle of concert performances and stopped performances midstream to share his philosophical views about everything from the music industry, fashion, politics and humanity. He's turned interviews upside down, he's shared his frustrations with the Paparazzi and has even announced his run for Presidency in 2020. On top of that he dated stripper Amber Rose and eventually married and has two children with Kim Kardashian who was catapulted into the limelight because of her sex-tape with Ray J. Most recently West cancelled the rest of his Saint Pablo tour dates before being hospitalized at the UCLA Medical Center for sleep deprivation and exhaustion. Through all of this, and more times than not, West has expressed very lucid thoughts on everything from capitalism, politics, human/civil rights, religion, the music/fashion industry, relationships and etc. Oftentimes his delivery is questionable. The very best interview I've seen was with Zane Lowe for BBC Radio.

"I've been sent here to give y'all my truth even at the risk of my own life, even at the risk of my own success, my own career. I've been sent here to give y'all the truth."
-Kanye West-

I think in order to gain a sense of where Kanye West is often coming from it's important for us to consider, and strive to understand, the perspective of a Creative. Although the content and contributions may be different, as a Creative, there is not much of a difference between Michael Jackson, Phyllis Hyman, Dave Chappelle, Nina Simone, Basquiat, Sly Stone, Lauryn Hill, Jimmy Hendrix, Zora Neale Hurston, Richard Pryor, Marvin Gaye and many others. To be a Creative and simultaneously exist within a racist/sexist entertainment industry that seeks to capitalize off of ones intellectual property is very difficult to cope with. Many have literally lost their mind. Others became drug addicts and alcoholics. Some left America while otherswalked away and became a recluse. Many died here, from a broken heart.

Being a Creative requires a person to think differently about life and solve problems in a new way. In order to do this, Creatives face fears, self-doubt and take risks that many people don't. Thought leaders; Creatives are ambassadors of an uncharted territory the world has yet to discover and fully appreciate. They are the subject matter experts of the unknown. To be this kind of person we must be open to inspiration at all times. Inspiration that often defies social norms and conflicts with the status quo. As a painter that may mean working countless hours and through sleepless nights to finally unveiling a social justice painting at a gallery owned by the very people who've fought against it. As an actor that may mean turning down the highest paid role you've ever received and Grammy shoo-in because it conflicts with your core values. As a musician that may putting your career and family security on the line to fight getting out of a record contract. As a fashion designer or model it may mean walking the long hard road of independent slow money instead of selling out your image, and images, to the highest bidder. All of these are life decisions that people often take for granted that Creatives have to make. There are many times I've literally been in my recording studio all night. There are many times I've been stirred out of my sleep in the middle of the night with an idea that I immediately start writing about. Many of these articles and chapters in my books are the result of this process. Being a Creative is like being on call from the universe because inspiration is a round-the-clock devotion to work. Although the beauty of what we manifest is timeless, the backstory, blood, sweat, tears and hours of dedication that often goes into forging such beauty is something many never see. What many also don't see is the stress, frustration and physical/social strain. As I've said, many Creatives have always strived to find various methods to cope with this in a society that tries to quantify, package, sell and often simultaneously marginalize, genius. West is not known for having a history of drug use or alcoholism. Aside from past lovers, he has not been associated with any women except his wife. The question many of us should be asking is how has he coped? I would argue that what we've seen from his off-the-cuff interviews, public meltdowns and concert rants is not him simply venting or throwing a tantrum. I would also argue that this medium has become his coping mechanism; a platform he's learned to use as an outlet and form of therapy.

There's an earthly gift and worldly curse that comes along with being a Creative. On one had you may be gifted to write the most beautiful poetry or paint the most brilliant picture the world has ever seen about love, yet be companionless or experience some of the most tumultuous relationships a person could imagine. Creatives are some of the most complex, sophisticated people to understand and the perimeters of a world always proves to be a societal box not large enough to contain their spirit. To paraphrase what Dave Chappelle once said, it's easy to call someone crazy. It's dismissive. It doesn't require you to examine anything they're saying or what's behind them acting the way they do. Maybe the environment West, and countless other Creatives have been in, is a little sick. If that is even part of our conclusion, we must ask ourselves what can we do to teach them, about healthy ways to disengage or healthy coping skills to thrive? I challenge all of us to not just consider that but strive to actively seek solutions; the mental, physical and socioeconomic health of our growing Millennial and Alpha generation depends upon that.

Pray-err

Sometimes people use prayer as an excuse to not get up and do something about a situation. Sometimes what we believe is in God's hands is really in our hands. If it's obviously on our mind, and in our heart, then it's most likely in our hands too.

Petty Joyner Kersee

The most athletic preschooler in my class is a 4 year old girl. She can naturally do all kinds of cartwheels, backbends, handstands and etc; I talked to her mom about getting her enrolled in some gymnastics classes. She's also THE FASTEST in the class. I'm talking about run circles around you FAST. Ten-foot head start still beat you FAST. Anyway, she dominates the boys in the class and be flossin on 'em when she does it. One of the boys can't stand it. If they're racing dude will stop when he knows she's winning and get mad. Today he was crying about it and said, "I don't like her." Lol I had to laugh to myself because it reminds me of being in elementary school with this quiet girl named Nicole who was the best artist and writer in the class. Her #2 pencil game was platinum and she won basically every art and writing contest without trying. I didn't like her because of that. Some of the other boys didn't like her either and she was cute too. Ya know, some of us males neeeeeever grow out of that.

5 Ways to Combat PTED
Post-Traumatic Election Disorder

Now that I've given it some time for the dust to settle I wanted to take a moment to offer some insights on this year's Presidential Election of Donald Trump.

For those of you who are unaware, I am a certified Machine Inspector for the BOE [Board Of Elections] in my County so I work at assigned polling sites during elections making sure the voting machines are operating properly, assisting citizens with their ballots and other things that come up. This is always an eye-opening experience and I get to meet and converse with people I probably wouldn't meet unless it were election day. So on November 8th I worked the polls from 5 am to 9 pm and like always, I wasn't disappointed. I'm sharing this to say that as a certified BOE Machine Inspector, a former 2013 County Legislature Candidate and now a Board Member for my City's Human Rights Commission, alot of my perspectives and talking points about the political process are from the inside looking out. This damn sure don't make me an expert, this experience just equips me with the knowledge to help others better understand realms that many of us don't enter, especially as Five Percenters. Anyway, PTED is a variation of PTSD [Post-Traumatic Stress Disorder]; a mental health condition that's triggered by a terrifying event -either experiencing it or witnessing it. In this case, that event was the 2016 Election. Basic symptoms include flashbacks, nightmares, mild to severe anxiety, depression, avoiding work, insomnia, irritability, loss of appetite, difficulty concentrating and uncontrollable thoughts about the event. From what I've seen every day published in the media, overheard in conversations and witnessed on social media are clear signs that this election was traumatic for many people and will continue to be traumatic for at least the next 4 years. Unlike most clinical diagnosis where the individual is labeled, PTED is the labeling of society -particularly its maladaptive political process. This is something we're all directly or indirectly dealing with and here are 5 ways to address it:

1.) According to exit poll data collected by Edison Research for the National Election Pool, which consists of ABC, CBS, NBC, CNN, Fox News, the Associated Press and the NY Times, almost 65% of white men and over 50% of white women voted for Donald Trump. A whopping 13% black men and only 4% black women voted for Trump. 93% black women supported Clinton. What's also important to consider is that more than 50% of the Baby Boomer and Traditionalist Generations voted for Trump while over 50% of Generation X and the Millennials voted for Clinton. This data, including data around voter's income and education, highlights the fact that there is not only a racial divide in this country. This country is also divided along gender, generational, education, income and political party lines. This country is divided regardless how cool Brad and your drinking buddies are during your tailgating parties or how close you are to Becky with the girl hair who cries and confides in you about her personal life. More than half of the time they've been smiling in your face but quietly rationalizing, and identifying, with Trump's misogynistic, xenophobic, racist rhetoric. The fact that over 50% white women voted for Trump but only 4% black women also says something about the Feminist Movement and to black feminists and their so-called white allies directly... Some of us were already aware of these divides and have been striving to communicate this to the masses of people for some time now. The problem is many of us didn't and probably still don't believe that certain segments of the American population are deliberately keeping us, people of color, women, low/middle class and the youth apart from their own socioeconomic equality. Hell, some of the 13% black men who voted for Trump are striving to keep people apart while they're being kept apart. The irony. This exit poll data, including looking at the voting data in the region, county and city where you live, gives you a very good critical analysis of the people, and their politics, around you. There's a great deal of mental stability having this knowledge.

2.) Trump supporters celebration victory of hate crimes, vandalism, embolden racism, sexism, religious fanaticism, homophobic violence is a stark reminder of this country's divide many of us have chosen to ignore. From Muslim women getting their hijab ripped off, Mexican children being taunted/bullied in Kindergarten, Black college students finding swastikas spray painted on university landmarks and black baby dolls with nooses around their neck, the elderly and disabled being ridiculed/assaulted and etc., this is and has always been a face of America. I say "a" face to imply that America is two-faced; it parades ideals of freedom, justice and equity for all citizens yet they've never lived up to them. It many cases it hasn't even tried. Considering this level of hatred and outright ignorance on the part of Americans I can only see heightened attacks on people of color, women, non-

Christians, the LGBTQ community, the disabled, our youth and anyone else who is not the face of a White Nationalist American Male status quo. Because of the exit poll data it also indicates that there are many allies/sympathizers with this status quo who are not white males. We need to protect ourselves, not out of fear, but because self defense is important. First we need to arm ourselves with knowledge to expand our awareness of the American landscape outside of the perimeters of the status quo. In addition to checking out my books at Quanaah Publishing, I encourage you to follow the blog of my Educator's Educator Life Justice: Black Consciousness on the 3rd Stone from the Sun. Next we need to literally arm ourselves by learning combative arts, survivalist skills and purchasing legal weapons. If we, especially our children, need to defend ourselves intellectually, emotionally and physically, we need to be prepared to do that without fear or hesitation.

3.) The Golden Era of Hip Hop was a time when the most creative, conscious and substantive rap music was born. This took place in the late 80's to the late 90's at the tail end of the Reagan Administration, during the Bush Administration and during the beginning of the Clinton Administration; the Crack, War on Drugs and Three Strikes You're Out Mass Incarceration Era. I am from Generation X so I lived through these Administrations and in hindsight can see how the various policies that came out of them effected the regional/local landscapes where I and many other black, brown and poor whites lived around the country. It wasn't good. Yet the social commentary of that time, via Hip Hop culture and rap music in particular, kept us consciously orientated and positively committed to one another in a way we hadn't seen since the 1960's inception of the youth-centric Five Percenters. The Black CNN as Chuck D called it, gave us life and life more abundantly during the most turbulent time of my generation. Because of this, I predict another cultural Renaissance. This also puts Generation X in vital position to help guide our peers, the Millennials and our Alpha Generation who may potentially experience similar policies under a Trump Administration with a Republican controlled House of Representatives and Senate. Our younger generation don't have the experience nor do they know what to expect. Even in light of what they're now witnessing with police terrorism and the post election white supremacy, many are still under the false impression that we're in a post-racial America. Half of the Baby Boomers and Traditionalists voted for this Administration or don't have the energy/ambition to lead so it's on us. If we don't model the core values, principles, collective work and responsibility and cooperative economics to lead the people it's a slim chance that it can happen. Additionally, realizing that our family is the vital building block of our communities, cities, regions and nation, we must reassess our views on relationships, motherhood, fatherhood and the role of the nuclear family. With more than half of all black, brown and poor white Millennials and Alpha Generation born out of wedlock, "Family First" must be our living motto, regardless how radical a change we'll need to make to our rugged individualistic, career woman and bachelor pad lifestyles. Our future literally depends on us.

4.) Regardless of our reaction to the election results, we must be willing and able to respond. For those of us who are protesting to raise awareness about the flaws of the Electorate College, Trump being elected or any other thing we're dissatisfied with about this government I commend and encourage you to also demonstrate this disapproval financially. There are businesses, organizations and agencies who share your sentiments, reciprocate your support and amplify these same ideals. Many were founded specially to do this! They are allies and a necessary connective base to help redirect the resources, build the institutions and transform the policies of this government.

5.) Now is not the time to be investing a bunch of energy trying to convince people about Trump's incompetence, his wife being an Amber Rosian FLOTUS or how ignorant his children are. Energy is better directed at striving to get together with people of like minds who are striving to help each other out.

Let me repeat, HELPING EACH OTHER out. Some of the key words during these next 4 years are: Collaboration, Partnership, Family, Community, Youth Advocacy, Localism, Volunteerism, Entrepreneurship, Alternative Energy, Underserved, Social Capital, Trades, Optimal Health, Investment, Consensus, Savings and Residual Income. There are others yet these are some vital ones to conceptualize and add to our language. We will need every one of them!

In closing I want to again remind all of you that this isn't the Rapture. Without a doubt we are going to have some tough times ahead of us, yet to weather any storm we must be willing and able to rise above our petty differences and unify. It seems like this election has forced many of us to realize this. I have confidence in our ability to work it out and I'm here, as I've consistently been, to add on. If you're striving to reach me directly my email is: atlantisbuild@gmail.com

Conditions

Instead of trying to force people, especially youth, to think more creatively it's easier to transform the conditions of the environment to nurture creativity.

About the Author

S. Quanaah (Saladin Q. Allah) is a Creative Artist and Therapeutic Recreation major who attended Central State University in Wilberforce, Ohio, a Historically Black College and University (HBCU). He has over two decades of journalist, community outreach and youth advocacy experience. During his experience as a journalist, Saladin's social commentary has been published in print and online in a wide range of publications and websites worldwide. His niche website A.S.I.A., where he writes bimonthly articles, has achieved a #1 Google page ranking and a peak global web traffic of 119,874 visitors per month. Saladin has written over 250+ articles, published fifteen books. As a Creative Artist he has performed Hip Hop, Poetry and Spoken Word at various venues and produced/recorded 4 full length albums; Brothers from Another Planet, The Emerald Tablet, Kontact and

Tapestry of Love. In 2011 A.S.I.A. was ranked one of the Top 100 Websites by United Black America Online.

In 2014 he was globally cited as a subject matter expert on Hip Hop Artist Jay-Z's cultural affiliations and in 2015 he founded and hosts Atlantis Build Talk Radio; a unique blend of informed commentary, music and interviews about the science of everything in life. As a community organizer and youth advocate he worked as program consultant for the History Channel Series Gangland episode 'The Hidden Valley Kings' and has created numerous projects, programs and initiatives that support the positive growth and development of youth and families worldwide. Saladin is a Human Rights Commissioner for the City of Niagara Falls, NY, a Resident Leader for the ReNu Niagara Create a Healthier Niagara Falls Collaborative, a Highland Community Revitalization Committee Board Member, Senior Program Facilitator and Parent Advocate for the STYA (Successfully Transitioning Youth to Adolescence) Program, a Preschool Teacher for the Niagara Falls Housing Authority's Universal Pre-Kindergarten Program and he tours as a Public Speaker.

For further information, you may visit his website A.S.I.A. at: www.atlantisschool.blogspot.com or by Googling "Atlantis Build."

www.atlantisschool.blogspot.com

www.ingramcontent.com/pod-product-compliance
Lightning Source LLC
Chambersburg PA
CBHW060253290526
45789CB00001B/310